THEY CAME TO Jerome

The Billion Dollar Copper Camp

ABOUT THE AUTHOR

Herbert V. Young was born in 1887 at Brushwood Manor, his parents' Arizona homestead. It was located 15 miles north of the village of Phoenix, in what is now Scottsdale.

After finishing a business college course, Young engaged in secretarial work. From 1912–1955, Young was secretary to the general manager of Jerome's United Verde Copper Company (purchased by Phelps Dodge Corporation in 1931).

He started writing in his seventies, drawing upon 43 years of experience in the development and decline of Jerome's mining operations. His two books about Jerome's mining history were published by the Jerome Historical Society: *Ghosts of Cleopatra Hill* (1964) and *They Came to Jerome* (1972).

In 1983, Northland Press of Flagstaff, Arizona published *Water by the Inch,* Young's reminiscences about his pioneer family and boyhood adventures on their desert homestead.

Young was a founding member of the Jerome Historical Society and served as its historian from 1953 until his death in 1988. He donated his papers and photographs to the Jerome Historical Society, which has archived them as The Herbert V. Young collection.

They Came to Jerome

The Billion Dollar Copper Camp

by Herbert V. Young

JEROME HISTORICAL SOCIETY
Jerome, Arizona

BOOKS BY HERBERT V. YOUNG

Ghosts of Cleopatra Hill

They Came to Jerome

Water by the Inch

© 1972 by Herbert V. Young

Second Printing, 1984
Third Printing, 1989
Fourth Printing, 2000 with new introduction and index

Published and distributed by—
Jerome Historical Society, Inc.
PO Box 156
Jerome, AZ 86331

Cover design—Sullivan Santamaria Design, Inc.
Index—Douglas R. Parker

Library of Congress
Catalog Card No. 72-87037

Printed in the United States of America

To the memory of
HERBERT V. YOUNG, JR. 1920–1944

First Lieutenant
United States Army Corps

CONTENTS

ILLUSTRATIONS

Note: All photos, except those specifically credited in the text, are from the author's private collection, now owned by the Jerome Historical Society.

FOREWORD

Because I grew up in the neighboring county seat of Prescott, *They Came to Jerome* evokes a thousand poignant memories. I recall wryly a disastrous high school football game on Jerome's field of crushed smelter slag in which we were on the short end of a score approximating 100–0; more pleasurably do I remember golf at the Verde Valley Country Club whose fairways—thanks to the Company—had far better turf than we enjoyed.

While grammatically unacceptable, the highway sign that boasted "The Most Unique City in America" well typified this ruggedly independent and self-reliant community. Jerome represented the quintessence of the entrepreneurial system in every phase of its life, from the Company down to the one-man grocery store, and would be anathema to today's social planners. However, the same rough and ready measures achieved prompt and effective community benefits that would get bogged down in the administrative red tape we now accept as God's will.

Herb Young possesses the personal knowledge to bring to his readers the unashamed gusto of a colorful era, and the skill to permit the story to speak for itself. It is my hope that this book will bring the same pleasure to those denied the experience of knowing Jerome firsthand that it does to those of us who did.

> Sherman Hazeltine
> Chairman of the Board
> First National Bank of Arizona

INTRODUCTION 2000

Jerome has experienced many changes since Herbert V. Young published *They Came to Jerome* in 1972. The ghost town has evolved into a prosperous tourist town and artist community. Most of the remaining buildings have been restored, and many new buildings constructed.

In 1953, the year Phelps Dodge closed the mines, concerned citizens formed the Jerome Historical Society. Hoping to save their beloved town through promoting tourism, they constructed the Mine Museum in the old Fashion Saloon and advertised Jerome as the "The World's Largest Ghost City." The Jerome Historical Society purchased many dilapidated buildings to preserve them from destruction. Society volunteers restored the old J. C. Penney building and called it "Spook Hall." Here, they held the annual "Spook" weekend where former residents returned to reminisce about Jerome's more prosperous times. The Douglas family donated the Douglas Mansion for the Jerome State Historic Park, which opened in 1965. In 1967 the National Park Service designated Jerome a "National Historic Landmark." Slowly, the dream of a prosperous community through tourism became reality. Today, Jerome's rich heritage, incredible views, and artistic community attract visitors from all over the world.

Beginning in the 1970's, the town's population began to rebound. Hippies and artists looking for a small community and inexpensive housing found Jerome a perfect refuge. Initially, the older residents of Jerome disapproved of these young people's lifestyles. Despite this, the young folks stayed and became valuable community members. Their artistic creations and shops helped attract tourists. They purchased and restored the run-down, vacant structures.

Life has returned to most of the buildings that were empty when *They Came to Jerome* was first published. The houses on the upper levels above Main Street ("Company Hill"), where mine officials once lived (page 8), no longer lie vacant. In 1973, Phelps Dodge leased the Victorian homes to the Jerome Centennial and Restoration Commission in partnership with the Jerome Historical Society for maintenance and restoration. Then, in 1988, Phelps Dodge sold them to a cooperative of residents. The Restoration Commission also leased the United Verde Apartments (page 44) in 1973. In 1993, private individuals purchased the building, renamed it the "Jerome Centre" and restored the apartments and commercial spaces. The fourth United Verde Hospital (pages 46 and 162) is now the Jerome Grand Hotel. The shell of the Little Daisy Hotel, (page 129) has been purchased and restored as a private residence. The Town of Jerome occupies the Clark Street Grammar School (page 133). The Hotel Jerome (pages 125, 129 and 130), now owned by the Town, is partially renovated into stores and studios. The old Jerome (later Mingus) High School (page 133) was sold to the Verde Exploration Company in 1972 and now houses offices and artists' studios. The Hull Avenue cribs (pages 8, 108, and 110) are among the few important structures that have been demolished in recent years.

The foliage, once completely destroyed by smelter smoke, has returned. In 1964, citizens air-seeded Ailanthus Altissima (Paradise) trees on Cleopatra Hill. These trees flourished and helped regenerate Jerome's damaged soil. Today, the once stark mountainside stands alive with green.

The Haven United Methodist Church remains Jerome's only active church. The congregation, which slipped to a low of two, has rebounded to around 60, enough to support a pastor. Although Mass is rarely performed in the Holy Family Catholic Church, the Catholic diocese still owns the structure and keeps it open to the public.

On page 7, Young wrote that one can reach Jerome via several roads. While this is true, some of these roads are very primitive. Visitors generally find their way to Jerome via Highway 89A, which traverses Mingus mountain and connects Prescott to Jerome and Cottonwood. From Cottonwood travelers can continue on 89A to Sedona, or take Highway 260 to Camp Verde and Interstate 17, which connects Phoenix and Flagstaff.

INTRODUCTION 2000

Jerome enters the new millennium as a vibrant town determined to maintain its heritage and prosperity. Although the population is under 500, Jerome gets more than a half-million tourists a year. Most people come to Jerome just for a day or two. Some, however, choose to stay and call this once "Billion Dollar Copper Camp" home.

Alene Alder, Archivist and Curator
Jerome Historical Society

New commercial building constructed in the 1980's on Main Street.
(*Jerome Historical Society*)

HERB YOUNG PHOTO.

Pine clad sentinel of Jerome and the Verde Valley, mighty Mingus rears its proud crest nearly 8,000 feet above sea level.

Prelude

Until it was stolen by some vandal with no respect for property, tradition, or history, there was a sign at the western approach to Jerome which informed the traveler that he was entering

THE MOST UNIQUE CITY IN AMERICA

The sign had been erected in Jerome's heyday by proud members of the city's chamber of commerce; and though the description was ultra-superlative the citizens believed that the message conveyed was obvious and unimpeachable fact. They had reason, for while few cities in America can be designated truly unique, this famed mining community in the Black Hills of Central Arizona is certainly one of those few.

The feat of clinging precariously to the steep and sliding slopes of a barren mountain is in itself sufficient to earn the designation "unique." But the element that really sets Jerome apart is the colorful and exciting saga of the men who burrowed deep in the mountains to create two of the world's great copper mines, the fame of which attracted people to this bonanza camp in an almost continuous stream for more than fifty years. They came from the town's beginning until its decline, men and women of many countries and classes, and they boosted, boomed and built the first lonely camp into a town and the town into a clamoring little city.

The story of the men who discovered, developed and protected the mines of Jerome has been told in GHOSTS OF CLEOPATRA HILL, this writer's first book relating to the Jerome scene. THEY CAME TO JEROME will deal specifically with the people of the town itself, those who in the fulness of their pride named it "The Billion Dollar Copper Camp" long before the ultimate billion in production had been attained; the people who attempted to direct the town's growth, feed, clothe and entertain its citizens, and time after time willed it

1

to rise from its ashes. And of course those who had no interest in the town aside from that which they could pry from it cannot be forgotten.

Events referred to in this book which have had prior coverage in GHOSTS OF CLEOPATRA HILL are presented in brief form and mentioned only for the sake of maintaining continuity.

The period in the history of Jerome covered herein begins with the first settlement at the base of Cleopatra Hill and ends with the great depression and the passing into other hands of the properties of Senator William A. Clark. Those were the days of pulsing and sometimes turbulent action of an intensity not experienced in the more settled days of the succeeding decades.

The interesting history of Jerome did not end there, and it is well worth recording: the recovery of the little city after four years of idleness of its only important industry; the years of another war, then another period of prosperity; sudden extinguishment; and finally the struggle of the few remaining inhabitants to build a new identity. But that must be the theme of yet another story.

The people of Jerome referred to their colony by differing designations. First it was called a camp. That was all it was and that name clung even while others intruded. It was incorporated as a town, and so it was officially known. But that name didn't satisfy the boosters who, as the community expanded, decided that it should be known as a city. In this book Jerome will be referred to by any one of the three designations even as the citizens referred to it.

I am happy to pay tribute to the many old timers, most of whom have ridden on into the night, who have given me their fascinating though often differing impressions of the early days, and to the pioneer editors of Jerome who, inspired by the excitements of the times and the seductive perfume of printers' ink spiced with smelter fume, left a record of people and events during the camp's metamorphosis from puling infant to bellowing giant. In Chapter 22 of this book I have endeavored to name those who have helped, also those writers and historians whose works have been consulted.

Those who have asked for such a book as this are beyond counting. The roots of the men and women who have come to Jerome and bided awhile are hard to pull. They like to look back. Some found adventure in the camp, perhaps in the turn of the wheel, or in wanderings in the canyons and valleys or on mountain trails and peaks. Some found a goal in trade, others in manual enterprise in smoking smelters or in dark and damp underground tunnels. Some found food for the mind, for through the years Jerome has harbored many men and women of intellect. Many established competences; a few found wealth. Numberless young men and women found romance.

But whatever the individual memories of those who lived in or close to Jerome, they are such as to bring a great many of them on pilgrimages back to their one-time hillside home, where with the smelters gone and cities far away the air is again free of fume and the mountain breezes blow sweet and clean.

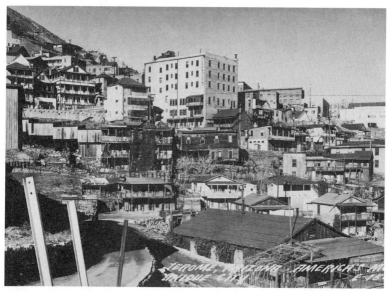

Houses cling haphazardly to the side of Cleopatra Hill, circa 1930.
(Jerome Historical Society, Anne Bassett Col.)

The first close-up view of Jerome as the traveler traverses the Hogback from the east, circa 1970. (Jerome Historical Society)

JEROME
POPULATION
15,000
10,000
5,000
1,000
GHOST CITY

Perspective

More than a century ago, after the first settlers had come to the Verde Valley and a military post had been established at Fort Verde, scouting parties traveling twenty miles up river saw on a hilltop near the stream the eroded ruins of a large Indian pueblo which had been abandoned hundreds of years before. Directly westward rolling hills climbed to high pine covered mountains.

Looming above the succession of ascending hills was a massive, craggy eminence, resembling in contour a huge crouching dog. North of it another high mountain stretched, against which in the nearer distance arose a tall cone, gray or chocolate or black or tan according to the angle of the sun's rays.

In later years these elevations, in the order given, were to be known as Mingus Mountain, named for two brothers who had a camp on its slopes; Woodchute Mountain, so called because a chute built of logs was constructed on its eastern side to guide timbers down to the mine level; and Cleopatra Hill, named for a mining claim at its southern base.

Across the river from the Indian ruins, now called Tuzigoot, was a dimly defined trail leading westward, traveled by deer and other animals but extending so far and so directly into the mountains as to indicate human origin and purpose. In the 1870's the first settlers at Peck's Lake near the ruins followed this trail into the pinelands and discovered that it ended at outcroppings of rich ores four miles from and two thousand feet above the river's level.

The ground surrounding these outcroppings was located as mining claims in 1876, and developed into the historic United Verde mine.

Down below the mine at the eastern foot of the Cleopatra cone there was ground with slopes less steep, and here a settlement was started. In 1883 the camp was given the name of Jerome.

At first the only way to reach the settlement was from Prescott by

Steps to nowhere.

Don't walk—climb. This way to the next street

way of Fort Verde, thence to the mining camp by foot or horseback. But soon rough wagon roads were built.

When William A. Clark's new smelter was blown in the latter part of 1894 the camp's estimated population was 500, mostly workmen. Then came a time of rapid building. Stores and rooming houses came quickly. Saloons with their gambling tables and entertainers led the pace. When the railroad reached Jerome in 1893 men began to bring their families. A school was established. In 1900 there were three church buildings with growing congregations. New mineral prospects were being worked. For a while in that period there were three newspapers.

The population of Jerome grew steadily until 1930, when the census takers counted nearly five thousand inhabitants. There were many more scattered in little settlements on the hills and in the canyons near by.

When the white man first came to the Black Hills a forest growth covered all of them. Today one sees no pines on Cleopatra Hill or Woodchute Mountain. The pine was cut for lumber and mine timbers, and the smaller growth was killed by acid fumes from the smelter and ore roasting pyres. The forest did not come back.

To quote a phrase that has been over-used, "You have to see Jerome to believe it." Travelers have declared it to be one of the few mountain towns on earth of any size that one can view in its entirety from forty miles away, airline, and from an elevation two thousand feet higher while one's feet are still on the ground. From the Mogollon rim one can look down across the Verde Valley and view its clustered buildings clearly. At night its lights twinkle like the lamps of a Christmas tree.

Down from the rim to Sedona, then to the Verde River, then upward to Jerome is an interesting and rewarding trip through the red rock formations for which Oak Creek Canyon is famous. One can travel now on paved roads which have replaced the rutty, rocky wagon trails of the early years. Approaching Jerome from the east through Walnut Gulch one sees how the people of the camp had to build their homes on the steep hillsides. With the top floor at street level, a house might be supported on stilts, either open to the winds or enclosed to form one or two more habitable floors. Traveling on one ascends a steep hill to the business section of Jerome.

The town can also be reached by roads from the west, north and south. All routes are graced by spectacular scenery.

From the Main Street trade center, buildings at one time flowed downward to the depths of Deception Gulch to the east, north to Bitter Creek, and to the west upward for several levels on the side of Cleopatra Hill. There were steps and stairways everywhere, some even now usable, some crumbling away. They climbed upward from Main Street to Clark, from Clark to Giroux, and on. Access for vehicles would be at one end of a street, turn around to come back. On the down slope of each roadway were retaining walls to hold the road beds in place.

In the central area of the business section, many of the buildings on the lower side of Main Street and on Hull Avenue directly below, and on into the Gulch, are gone, prey to the settling caused by unstable ground. But many of the old business buildings still stand, and the shells of many of the residences on the upper levels above Main Street are still there. These houses northward to the open pit area, where the mine officials lived, were owned by the Copper Company and were never sold to private individuals. They have been stripped of everything that could be salvaged—plumbing fixtures, doors and windows, maple floors. Storms have taken heavy toll. Inside the rooms one may find rock and mud, washed through rear doors by waters from heavy rains draining from the steep slope above.

The now vacant blocks on Main Street and Hull Avenue were once jammed with stores, saloons, rooming houses, restaurants. Crowded against the rear of still standing business buildings at the north end of Main Street, and within a hundred yards of Jerome's busiest street corners, were the "cribs," apartments built of brick, some of two stories, which once housed many of Jerome's madams and their girls. Across the street from these were several frame buildings put to the same use. The frame buildings are gone, but the curious visitor may still see the shells of the brick walled bordellos.

To illustrate the crazy wanderings of Jerome's streets, the accompanying chart shows their can-of-worms pattern, with names of the principal streets. This is not drawn to scale—it is condensed, but it shows what the surveyors, engineers and builders had to contend with in laying out a townsite on and in the steep slopes and gulches. Many short streets and byways are not shown.

During Jerome's life, extending over a period of nearly one hundred years as this is written, people came to Jerome from many parts of

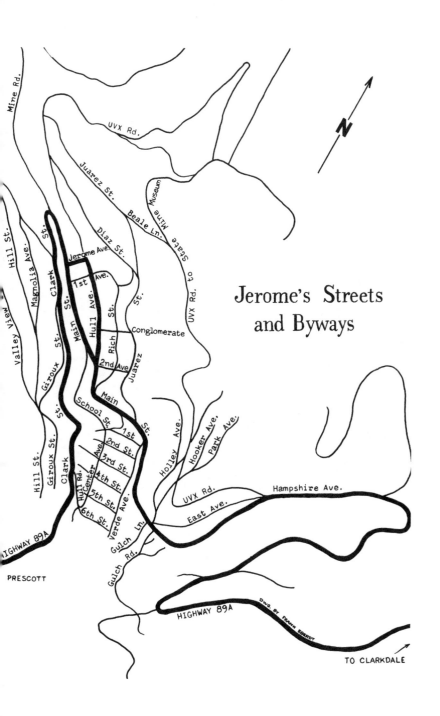

Jerome's Streets
and Byways

the globe. There were Europeans of a dozen ethnic groups. Men of the Orient came. From below Arizona's southern border there was a steady migration, as well as from every state in the Union. Canadians came in numbers.

When disaster finally struck and the last of Jerome's mines closed, the flow of travel was reversed, and the great majority of residents of the town went away. There were left only those few whose roots were too deep to sever, or who had no other place to go, and those thousands who slept in their vaults of caliche on the rocky hillside or in the green valley below.

Landslides destroyed part of Jerome's downtown in the late 1930's. The Kovacovich building, which once housed a grocery store, collapsed in February 1937. (Jerome State Historic Park)

Whence They Came

Literally, they came from all over. Within three decades after Clark's smelter began to make smoke the "maps" of thirty to forty countries could be seen in the faces of the people of Jerome.

The best time to have studied these faces would have been on a pay day. The sidewalks, saloons and stores were crowded with men, from sunrise to sunset, then from sunset to another sunrise, buying clothing and food, gambling, drinking and fighting. Occasionally a man might even have been seen depositing money in the bank.

In the earliest of Jerome's days men didn't seek Jerome in numbers; they were sought out, for then all that was known of the camp—and that by only a few—was that across some valleys and over some mountains there were a few men living in tents and doing some digging on some rich mining claims. When the United Verde Copper Company was organized in 1882 and plans laid for a smelter, the first need was to build roads, which called for men with strong backs and horny hands. Such men were found and brought in from other road construction projects.

After the Civil War immigration from Ireland had been heavy, and Irish workmen formed a high percentage of road gangs in the United States. When the camp's developers sought laborers to build a wagon road across the Black Hills to connect with one already built from Prescott across Lonesome Valley, the gang of nearly a hundred men they rounded up were mostly from Erin. A payroll of that period shows that all but a few bore Irish names. There were a small number of native born Americans, but only two names of Spanish origin. Wages were $2.50 to $3.00 a day. A burro was also on the roll—he got $1.00 a day.

The percentage of the workers of each nationality varied throughout the years, but in 1920, midway between the beginning of the United Verde operation and its ending, a nationality report compiled by the company's labor department showed that in a work force of 2200 the following nationalities were represented:

American, Austrian, Bulgarian, Canadian, Dutch, English, Finnish,. French, German, Greek, Irish, Italian, Mexican, Portuguese, Russian, Scottish, Scandinavian, Serbian, Slavic, Spanish, Swedish, and Welsh. There was also a miscellaneous classification.

In the compilation referred to, workmen of Mexican origin were of larger number than of any other race, approximately twenty percent. There were about as many classed as Americans. The Slavs came next in number, then the Spanish, Austrian, Italian and Irish, and the others in descending ratio. In the years that followed the percentage of Mexicans gradually increased until they composed about half of the work force.

The distribution of nationalities among the employees of the United Verde Extension Mining Company and the smaller mines of the district was in approximately the same proportion as at the United Verde.

A steady migration of east Europeans began after the railroad came to Jerome. Among the Slavic races represented in that group were Slovakians, Slovenes, Magyars, Croatians and Montenegrins, as well as the Serbians, most of whom were classed as Austrians on the mining company's payroll records as at that time their lands were under the domination of the Austro-Hungarian empire.

As immigrants became settled many sent back home for families or sweethearts. Others found wives in Jerome.

Around the turn of the century the east European workmen predominated in the foreign element, but in time the Mexicans overtook them.

Many of the immigrants who made their start in Jerome as laborers saved their money and became landlords, tradesmen or saloon keepers. Men of several nations were among the saloon operators. It is not known that the Chinese had any bars, but they did have their opium dens, frequently raided by the town officers. In the earlier days one saloon was operated by a Japanese.

Among the operators of merchandise establishments were Irish, Italians, Slavs, Hebrews and Armenians, but Americans predominated.

It was natural for the immigrants to form into language groups, and disagreements among the groups occurred at intervals. There were occasional battles, but not a great deal of blood was shed because of interracial animosities.

WHENCE THEY CAME

Only a few American Indians were employed at the mines and smelters. But they were often seen in the camp, where they came to sell baskets or pottery or just to sit on the curb and watch the antics of the paleface.

As the years passed and a younger generation became a factor in the life of the community, assimilation began, and the various groups began to intermingle in harmony. Many of the immigrants were anxious to accumulate competences of their own, and some succeeded. Others were anxious to have their sons and daughters take responsible positions in society, and financed their college educations or encouraged them to work their way through. In the Verde Valley and throughout Arizona communities, and in some instances in other states, names which became established in old Jerome are to be found in business and among the professions and the arts. There are doctors, dentists, lawyers, musicians, writers, architects, engineers, ministers, artists, actors, and members of almost every other profession or calling that could be named.

Jerome was a good example of the melting pot. It was an excellent training ground for the youth who aspired to go on and up. As the years eroded prejudices, men and women of different ancestries intermarried. The pride of origin gradually gave way to the realization, with pride, that they were Americans.

Further notes on Jerome's ethnic groups will be found in the Appendix to this volume.

Miners came from all over the world to work in Jerome's prosperous mines.
(Jerome Historical Society, Shen Col.)

13

How They Came—and Went

The earliest arrivals at the camp to be called Jerome could get there by only one established route—from Prescott to Fort Verde thence up river and mountain to the camp. They could either "hoof it" as many did, or if affluent ride a horse, mule or burro. Now the traveler can reach Jerome by highway from either of the four directions.

In 1882 and 1883 Frederick F. Thomas, for the newly organized United Verde Copper Company and with some aid from Yavapai County, built two wagon roads which served Jerome. The first one was over the mountain southwestward from the mine, connecting with the military and stage road from Prescott to Camp Verde at a point near the present-day Dewey. Elevations on this road ranged from 5,000 to 7,000 feet; it had some very steep grades, and when the snows of winter and the heavy rains of summer occurred there were periods when passage was impossible. So Thomas sought a route to rail with easier grades and lower elevations, and built a road north and northwest from Jerome to connect with the road from Prescott to Ash Fork.

In later years a road was built from Dewey through the little mining camp of Cherry Creek, meeting the one from Camp Verde to Jerome. The original military road through Copper Canyon was abandoned. Highway 79, the Black Canyon route, now passes through Copper Canyon, following approximately the route of the pioneers who settled at Clear Creek in 1865.

The Cherry Creek road was the outlet from the Verde Valley west until the building of Highway 89 Alternate in 1920. This follows generally the route of Thomas's first road, though the last section, with its entry into Clark Street, Jerome, was blasted from the steep wall of Hull's Canyon.

After Jerome became a good market for produce, wagon roads were built into the Oak Creek country, from which area one could also find his way into Flagstaff over two precarious routes, one up Schnebly

Hill eastward, the other by the notorious "switchback" road to the north, both leading to the high, forested plateau of the Mogollons.

The road from Flagstaff down Schnebly Hill to Oak Creek was the route by which some of the miners from Colorado, Utah and New Mexico reached Jerome. Walking from Flagstaff or Prescott to Jerome was not uncommon when the camp was young and its fame had begun to grow.

When the United Verde's first smelter was built in 1883, all materials were hauled in from Prescott or Ash Fork over the Mingus route, including the first smelting furnace. Multi-teamed freight wagons were used. There were heavy grades on the approach to the mines, when the broken saddle between Cleopatra Hill and Woodchute mountain had to be crossed. The grade was as steep as thirty percent in places, and coming up the wagon trains had to double up their teams and haul the loaded wagons one at a time over the hump. Heavy brakes operated with block and tackle were on all wagons, and to make sure there were no breakaways, behind the rear wheels of each wagon, dragged by chains and crosswise of the direction of the wheels, were twelve-inch-square sections of timber. These blocked the wheels when the wagons rolled back.

On the outward trip from the smelter site, to make safe the wagons loaded with copper matte on the steep down grade, the rear wheels were run into trough-like iron shoes, held in place under the wheels by chains attached to the frame of the wagon bed. These acted as skids to ease the wagon down to more level ground.

Thus were brought to Jerome all supplies and fuel for the furnace, and in this manner were hauled out the bars of copper matte. The grades of the second road to the north were easier, but in wet weather mired loads were not uncommon on the long haul to rail at Ash Fork.

When declining copper prices forced the closing of the little smelter in 1884, upkeep on the roads to Jerome ceased. The road northward was never used again, for in 1887 the Prescott and Arizona Central railroad—the so-called Bullock line—was built to Prescott from Seligman on the Santa Fe main line. The cost of this road, $300,000, was covered by Yavapai County bonds guaranteed by the territory. In the same year Frederick Tritle, former territorial governor and one of the organizers of the United Verde, leased the mine and smelter and attempted to resume the making of copper. In addition to renovating

Above: Burro teams delivered wood for Jerome's stoves and the smelter ore-roasting pyres.

Below: Teams of twenty mules and horses powered these freight wagons, which served Jerome and the mines before the first railroad came.

the mine and surface plant and installing a second furnace it was necessary to make extensive repairs on the road over the mountain to the railroad, an expense only partially borne by Yavapai County. Tritle's venture was financially disastrous.

The wagon road across Mingus was again, and finally, abandoned. The Cherry Creek road again became the only western outlet from the valley.

But traffic directly to and from Jerome by rail was only seven years away. In 1893 William A. Clark completed a narrow gauge railroad, the United Verde & Pacific, to connect Jerome with the new line being built from Ash Fork to Prescott and Phoenix. Immediately construction material for a new smelter began to roll in. So did people. Jerome boomed.

The new railroad was twenty-seven miles long. The first thirteen miles from Jerome Junction was over fairly level ground, but the last fourteen miles was blasted out of the rugged mountain. In that last stretch there were 187 curves and 28 bridges, according to Tom Jacobs, for many years a conductor on the line, and confirmed by George McMillan and George Haskins, pilots of the locomotives. The rails were only three feet apart; many of the curves were sharp, and the grades in places were steep. The rolling stock was all built to special order, the trucks for both the cars and the locomotives so constructed as to enable them to negotiate the radical curves. The engines were built for power, with no regard for speed; they functioned well, and hauled a tremendous tonnage of freight, all of which had to be transferred from broad to narrow gauge cars at the Junction.

The United Verde & Pacific became known as "the crookedest railroad in the world." It was also called "the corkscrew line." Those of us who traveled the line had no doubt that it was correctly described by either name.

The trains reached the end of their journey high above the main section of Jerome and above the smelter. When the passengers left the train they found that one of the most exciting parts of their journey was yet to come—the half-mile "slide" down the steep road to the town's center. A horse drawn rig, an open air vehicle with several wooden seats, awaited them. For many years "Boney" Hughes—Charles E. Hughes of the Ewing & Hughes livery and transfer operation—drove this rig. Boney had a wry sense of humor, and he delighted in sending

Above, one of the little narrow gauge locomotives which served Jerome for a quarter century. George McMillan, in center of crew of three, drove it and also, below, the "mighty Mallet" shown on its first trip to Jerome in 1920.

his team downward at a frightening speed. Strong men cursed; frequently a woman passenger would express her fright with a piercing scream. All hung on for dear life. But Boney always got them down safely, advising any who had enough breath left to protest that he had never killed a passenger yet.

In 1912 Senator Clark financed, and the Santa Fe built, a standard gauge line from Cedar Glade Station (later to be named Drake) on the Ash Fork-Phoenix road down rough country and the Verde River canyon to Clarkdale, enabling the United Verde to receive material for the construction of its huge new smelter. Shortly afterward the building of a railroad toward Jerome was begun. This too was quite an engineering feat. The first section from Clarkdale to Hopewell ore haulage tunnel was begun in 1913 and completed in 1915; it connected the ore haulage tunnel with the smelter. Power for the construction equipment was still the mule. This line was extended to Jerome in 1919. Passenger service was inaugurated in 1920, but motor car competition brought about its abandonment in 1925.

When it came to curves the Clarkdale-Jerome line (named the Verde Tunnel & Smelter and by local wags called the "Very Tired & Sleepy") could furnish competition to the United Verde & Pacific. It climbed two thousand feet in less than four miles airline, requiring with all its twistings and turning eleven miles of track. It had sixty-five curves, plus switchback assemblies.

In 1920 the narrow gauge line to Jerome was abandoned and its rail and equipment scrapped.

The United Verde Extension added to the railroad mileage in the Verde Valley when it began construction of its smelter and town south of Cottonwood in 1917. The new town was first named Verde then changed to Clemenceau in honor of the famed war leader, with whom James S. Douglas had become acquainted while doing Red Cross work in France in World War I. A broad gauge line connected the new smelter with the Santa Fe road at Clarkdale, and a branch was built for ore haulage to the portal of the Josephine tunnel which, similar to the Hopewell tunnel, led from underground workings to an opening on the hillside.

Around the turn of the century the United Verde acquired some of the first electric locomotives ever built for underground mining, replacing mules. They were also used for hauling slag to the dump.

Above: Dr. Lee A. Hawkins with his and Jerome's first automobile.

Below: The Hendey car, only one of its name ever made. Built by Arthur Hendey, superintendent of the Copper Chief, in the mine's machine shop.

They were odd looking little things, called saddlebacks. The mine was completely electrified eventually.

Three installations for a different kind of transportation were made in different periods near Jerome. After William A. Clark had acquired the United Verde mine and had begun smelting copper in the original little plant, he and his superintendent J. L. Giroux studied a means of avoiding the irksome haul of freight between the mine and the easier grades of the Yaeger Canyon road. The outcome was a six-mile-long aerial tramway from the smelter across the saddle on the western slope of Mingus mountain known then as now as the Summit. It was completed in 1891. The cables were supported by towers built of pine timber. Little cars with a capacity of about three hundred pounds were carried on the cables, their movement powered by a steam engine at the smelter furnaces. Coke and other supplies were moved from a Yaeger Canyon station to the smelter, and copper matte was sent out the same way.

The tramway operated fitfully, with many halts. A windstorm finally wrecked a part of it and it was not rebuilt.

A few years later Clark built another tramway under different circumstances. When some good ores were developed in his Iron King claim south of Jerome he built a little smelter there and a mile long aerial tramway to deliver the ores to it. As the smelter was several hundred feet lower than the mine, the tramway operated successfully on gravity power, the loaded cars drawing back the empty ones. It was in steady use until the ores which could be profitably smelted played out four years later.

When the United Verde Extension made its rich strike it had ores to market. In 1915 an ore bin was erected on the V. T. & S. road near Hopewell, a trail from the mine was built and a train of burros engaged to pack ores down to it. Quite a number of railroad cars were loaded in this manner and shipped to the Phelps Dodge smelter at Douglas. With the ores running around forty percent copper the returns were soon sufficient to finance the building of an aerial tramway to replace the burros. This line was about a mile in length and served until the new Clemenceau smelter commenced operation in 1918 and rail shipments of ores via the Josephine tunnel commenced.

A small airfield was built in the late twenties by volunteer labor near Clemenceau on land donated by the United Verde Extension.

This was improved in 1932 by William A. Clark III, the Senator's grandson, who planned to establish a school for the training of flyers. His partner in this venture was Jack Lynch, who had been an instructor of Lindbergh when the future Lone Eagle was first testing his wings. Their planning came to an abrupt end when both were killed when their plane crashed during a blind flying practice flight. The field, now owned and operated by the City of Cottonwood, is well maintained and well used, though it never has had scheduled air service.

Until about 1920 good use had been found for horses and mules in construction work and hauling around the mines and smelters; then the animals were replaced by motorized equipment.

But one beast of burden remained around for a long time—the burro—and this chapter should not be closed without a tribute to that ugly, tough, scruffy and noisy little beast which has been a genuine benefactor of man for thousands of years. In early Jerome the burro was a familiar sight, packing in firewood and delivering all types of merchandise from groceries to lumber. Finally, when his services were no longer required, he was turned loose to roam at will. How we used to curse him when he despoiled our lawns, trampled our flower beds, ate the flowers, and tore asunder the fabric of night and demolished slumber by his horrendous braying. We're not often bothered with him nowadays; most of those remaining in this western land are treasured as pets. We're glad that now they may romp in what to them must be elysian fields instead of being poked over sand, cactus and rocks.

So, you ugly, stubborn, patient, trumpet-voiced friend of the pioneers, enjoy your respite from toil. We old timers miss you; we'd even be glad to hear you sing to us again.

What They Saw as They Came

They climbed the mountain not only because it was there, but because they were eager to learn what was on the other side.

While they came to Jerome from all directions, most of them arrived from the west, first over a twisting, climbing trail from Prescott, later over a rocky wagon road, and eventually by way of the crooked little narrow gauge railroad from Jerome Junction on the Ash Fork to Phoenix line. The scenic grandeurs which they saw as they came, and the picturesque camp at the end of the line, were the subjects of narratives by thousands of enthusiastic visitors—journalists and laymen alike—some soaring to epic proportions.

Presented here are impressions of two early day journalists, one of whom made the trip to Jerome by horse power, the other by rail. The first is extracted from an article placed by Governor Frederick A. Tritle in one of his scrap books; it was clipped from a Prescott newspaper, probably the *Courier*, in the spring of 1883. This expresses well the awe and enthusiasm aroused in the breast of a starry-eyed reporter by the wonders he observed during a carriage trip over the Black Hills range. When this trip was made the wagon road from the United Verde mine to Prescott was not quite completed, though passable for a light rig. The following is a condensation.

> The trip to the United Verde mine is made by a carriage ride of not over four hours from Prescott. Six miles from Prescott you reach Lonesome Valley, and then the road branches off across the valley to the hills. The trip across the valley to the hills is tiresome, but after the foothills are reached the remainder of the trip is made all the more enjoyable by contrast with what is past. Winding around through the lower hills, timber clad and rugged, the road follows a ravine or canyon, with the scenery ever changing and varied, up toward the higher mountains and dark, beetling cliffs.
>
> The difficulties which the labor and ingenuity of the road builders have overcome are remarkable. Winding its tortuous course, now circui-

23

tously, now in a zigzag way up the mountain sides, the road proceeds toward the summit. Looking back the view is striking in the extreme; the hills and mountains around Prescott can be plainly seen; the bald and rugged rocks, the timbered and grass clothed hills in the distance with the barren waste between, present a wondrous picture.

But the half has not been told. When the 7,000 foot summit has been reached, and the visitor turns his face toward the east, a vision of Nature's grandeur meets the gaze—so wondrous, so beautiful, and so impressive, that he stands in spell-bound silence eagerly drinking in the scene which is sufficiently powerful to excite the most stolid observer. Words fail in description. The writer has never seen the view equalled. In one grand panoramic view is found combined the wonders of the Sierras, of the Yellowstone, of the Yosemite, and the pastoral scenes of New England, blended in peaceful and harmonious effects.

Standing on this elevated point and looking down upon the valley of the Verde, with the river visible for miles like a beautiful ribbon of silver winding in and out among green fields and pleasant groves, while rising in the background the terraced red rocks, so wondrous in their formation and color, extending back and beyond the river for miles, reflect the rays of the sun with curious mirages and pleasing contrasts—gazing on such a scene, so peacefully harmonized from such a position, on the summit of grand mountains, with Arizona's cloudless sky for a canopy, one's feelings are inexpressible. The place is well worth a visit, even a pilgrimage from afar.

In 1899 Paul Hull, editor and publisher of *The Arizona Graphic* of Phoenix, made a trip to Jerome and was inspired to write of it. He came on the narrow gauge United Verde & Pacific railroad, and he was impressed with both the trip and what he found at the end of it. Part of his article follows.

Jerome, one of the earth's richest treasure houses, occupies a flight of steps on the eastern slope of one of Arizona's "black hills." It is the home of the 19th century cliff dwellers. Its homes and business buildings cling to the precipitous sides of the mountain like swallows' nests. Your neighbor to the rear, in Jerome, can't look into your back windows, although he can look down your kitchen chimney from his front porch. It is a city of magnificent distances, but not in the same sense as Washington. It has found foothold on a mountain side, 2000 feet above the valley of the Verde, and not even a burro can climb the hill except by the "switch back" method. From its dizzy height is presented a scene of splendid solitude—of magnificent loneliness. So vast is the map spread before the eye that the Verde river amidst its fertile fields is but a silver line in a ribbon of green, faintly accented on the somber and tumbled bosom of the desert. The vision finds no rest until it meets the painted walls of the canyon, forty miles to the east, and it then seems but a step to the snow-capped summits of the San Francisco peaks, fifty miles beyond.

If the visitor to Jerome isn't seasick from his ride through the hills, he is insured of sufficient strength of stomach to stand the sulphur bath through which he passes between the railroad station and the hotel, 300 feet below. Jerome is the eastern terminus of the United Verde & Pacific railroad, which branches from the Santa Fe, Prescott & Phoenix road north of Prescott. In its construction, cuts and fills were evidently left out of calculation, and it follows the sides of the hills in a course so tortuous that it makes the B. & O. look like a straight line in comparison. It is twenty-six miles, as the road goes, from Jerome to the main line, but a bird could possibly fly it in a few minutes. In twelve of these miles of track eighty-four curves occur, many of them on the most acute crack-the-whip angles.

The road enters Jerome high above the town, the great United Verde smelter, and the fields of "roasting" ore at an elevation of 5,551 feet. Main Street in Jerome, with its hotels and saloons, is 350 feet below the station. When the traveler enters the 'bus, which is a species of mountain wagon, the driver clucks to the team, the horses stiffen their forelegs, seat themselves in the harness breeching and slide down at an angle of about 45 degrees. The descent is usually made without accident. When the wind is not propitious, and that is seldom, the descent is made through the sulphur fumes arising from the roasting beds, that rack the lungs and thoroughly fumigate the body. Infectious diseases are unknown. Bedbugs, fleas, and such vermin are rare and such of it as survives necessarily comes from the valley. Nothing can enter the town alive from the railroad station but healthy mammals.

Jerome, being a creature of the great copper mine, is a mining town, but it is typical of the mines only in the masculine character of its population. Physically it is rapidly becoming one of the most substantially constructed towns in the world. When a tent or shack disappears its place is taken by a fire proof building of the latest construction.

Fire has been Jerome's blessing as well as its curse. In 1898 the town was totally destroyed by fire, and in May 1899 a considerable portion was again burned. The business buildings put up since then are of the most substantial character, and are as nearly fireproof as stone, brick

Above: Jerome's depot bus with passengers ready for the "slide" down the steep hill to Jerome's center. "Women screamed; strong men cursed."

Delivering groceries from Alex Lyon's store c. 1910. By wagon for the more level streets, by pack horse for the steeper roads and trails.

and concrete can make them. The "company" has nearly completed a large brick hotel building, which seems to anticipate a population in Jerome of 20,000. The hospital building, maintained by the employees, is a first class structure of ornamental design. The company's store is of brick, three stories in height on one street and four on the other. It is the largest business house in town. The Connor hotel and many of the saloon buildings are of a permanent character. The "Fashion" saloon and gambling house is of concrete and cost about $20,000. High up on the hill above the business section, are many handsome new residences, chiefly of wood, most of them of the cottage and villa style, showing abundance of roof and ornamental plate glass windows.

The democratic proportion of saloons to churches maintains—16 to 1—but the ratio will not long endure. The Congregational society has the only church building, but the Catholics are building, and the Episcopalians propose to build.

The "king pin" of Jerome is H. J. Allen, the financier of the United Verde mine. He is not only a man of money, but he is a society "swell" and a politician. He lives in a handsome house, high up on the hill, near the mine. He affects high stepping horses and low-necked carriages, although a balloon would be more serviceable for carrying purposes in Jerome. He would have a butler in pumps, if he dared, but Jerome wouldn't stand for it. I knew Mr. Allen was a politician as long ago as last February, when the Arizona legislature was in session. There were bills, affecting mines, under consideration in the house committees. One day Mr. Allen came to Phoenix. He seemed to have no particular mission. He just brought his knitting along and came to visit. He drank a little tea with his neighbors, and the next day after his arrival the house chaplain was excused from duty for the day and those three bills were taken out of committee and killed quicker than scat.

Jerome has many virtues that a stranger would never suspect and it is painfully peaceable, when the number and kind of its male population is considered. I saw only one drunk man and he lay on the sidewalk all afternoon and nobody kicked him or stole his hat. And this man had a right to be drunk, if any such right exists. He was a polander and it was pay day.

After Jerome had gained fame as one of the richest mining camps in the world, many other writers visited Jerome and published articles either in praise or condemnation of it. References to some of these are made in other chapters of this book.

Main business block 1896

Jerome Sets Sail

When in 1876 the history of the camp which was to become Jerome began, the United States was celebrating the one hundredth anniversary of the signing of the Declaration of Independence. In that year nine men and one woman recorded location notices for the ten claims and three millsites in Arizona's Black Hills which six years later were absorbed by the United Verde Copper Company.

In 1876 Ulysses S. Grant, hero of the war between the states, was serving his second term as president. His appointee A. P. K. Safford was governor of the Territory of Arizona. In this year too, General George Armstrong Custer and his troops were massacred at the Little Big Horn in Montana by the Sioux led by Chief Sitting Bull, and Alexander Graham Bell spoke into a crude instrument the world's first telephone message. The population of the United States was 45,000,000; Arizona's white population was 11,000, including 2,500 residents of Yavapai County. A school census showed Arizona had 2,900 children of school age—that is, between six and twenty-one years—and of these 340 could read and write!

When Frederick F. Thomas began preparations in 1882 for the building of the United Verde's first little smelter, men other than laborers began to arrive in the camp. George W. Hull came, acquired ground where much of the town was subsequently built, helped lay out a townsite, and sold surface rights to building lots. Newcomers located more claims, and the surrounding mountains were soon pocked with assessment diggings. Jake and Bill Mingus established a saw mill on their mountain, and found quick sale for all the lumber they could produce. This, with the supplement of canvas and tarpaper, was used in the construction of enough housing to shelter the growing population. By the time the one furnace smelter was ready to go in 1883, the camp possessed a blacksmith shop, a saloon, a restaurant, a barber shop, Hull's general store, and a lodging house or two. Up at the mine and smelter the United Verde had its own boarding house and dormitories.

The first little boom lasted only two years. When the smelter ceased production in 1884, the camp became almost depopulated and so remained until Montana millionaire William A. Clark obtained control of the United Verde and resumed production in 1888. There was a brief revival when in 1887 Frederick A. Tritle operated briefly. The decade ended on a wave of optimism.

The town was named in 1883 and a post office established with Frederick F. Thomas, who with Tritle organized the United Verde, its first postmaster.

With the advent of Clark the camp began to boom again. Joseph L. Giroux, an experienced miner from Montana, was installed as superintendent, and soon Jerome's streets were ringing with the news that a real bonanza was in the making. Giroux opened up the first of the great orebodies which were to keep the United Verde among the top producers of copper for more than fifty years.

In 1891 Jerome had the first of a number of serious epidemics; typhoid fever caused a number of deaths.

The little railroad ran three trains a day. A settlement grew up at Jerome Junction; a considerable force was needed to transfer materials to the narrow gauge cars. A hotel was built there, several residences, and of course a saloon was among the first of the enterprises.

Clark also established a brick plant at Jerome Junction, which supplied brick for his smelter and residence and business buildings.

Hull was the first man to establish a general store in Jerome, but with the coming of the smelter there came others. Deane and Horace Merrill opened a general store, as did Con O'Keefe. Doane Merrill was appointed Jerome's third postmaster in 1892. With the beginning of the Clark operation came the T. F. Miller Company, which was to dominate merchandising in Jerome for decades. T. F. Miller, whose son Walter managed the enterprise, was a brother-in-law of Clark, and by benefit of nepotism unlimited capital was available. The first Miller store was at "The Bend" on the way up the hill to the smelter; its stone building was later used as a warehouse and still stands. Other businesses were also at the Bend, including Dan Shea's saloon.

More people flocked in following the widely published news that in the final months of 1894 the United Verde smelter poured 11,000,000 pounds of copper which contained the almost incredible riches of 7,500,000 ounces of silver and $1,500,000 in gold. From these results grew the legend, which lived long after its allegation no longer applied, that the silver and gold in the United Verde ores paid all operating expenses and left the returns from the copper pure profit.

In the remaining years of the nineteenth century Jerome strained, hustled and bustled. New money continued to flow in to finance more mining ventures and other enterprises, and there was a scramble for business sites on Main Street and Hull Avenue, with rapidly increasing prices. Law enforcement of a firm type came with the appointment of Jim Roberts as deputy sheriff for Jerome and the establishment in the town of a justice court.

While no accurate list of the business establishments in the town prior to 1895 is available, we do have such information beginning with 1895 when Herbert Eugene Wilcox established *The Jerome Chronicle,* the first of several newspapers the town was to have during the next quarter of a century. In that year L. C. Hughes was territorial governor; former governor Frederick A. Tritle was Yavapai County's recorder; Robert E. Morrison of Prescott was district attorney, and George C. Ruffner was sheriff. George W. Hull was taking time off from his business and mining activities to represent the Verde Valley in the territorial legislature.

The effect on the community of the United Verde's operation in 1895, the first full year of operation of the new smelter, was stimulating and a portent of prosperity to come. A million dollars a month clear profit to William A. Clark from his new found bonanza was the popular estimate, and the figures of the statisticians seemed to bear this out. The Black Hills mines were featured in many publications, and the publicity was shared by the bustling, bursting camp itself. People looking for mining claims to develop legitimately, or to use for wildcat promotions, continued to flow in.

Down in the valley about all of the land which could be irrigated, and much that could not, had been homesteaded, and water appropriated from the Verde river and from various copiously flowing springs. From one of the largest of these springs flowed the water which irrigated a fine fruit and vegetable ranch operated by partners A. G. Haskell and ·John Kirwagen. The United Verde bought this ranch for its water in 1910; when Clarkdale was founded in 1912 the water was appropriated for the town and the Haskell spring still remains the source of Clarkdale's water supply.

In this period the female population of Jerome increased rapidly, and the number of children also. In 1895 Jerome's little frame school house, with two rooms, had an enrollment of sixty-four children. One teacher took care of the lot.

There were several saloons in the three block area of Jerome's business section, others on Jerome Avenue, the short street extending to Hull Avenue between the Fashion saloon and the Connor Hotel. Names shown in the *Chronicle* included the Stone Saloon of Dave Connor, on the site later occupied by the Connor Hotel, the Ward & Cole saloon, and the Star. Dan Shea's saloon at the Bend was Dan's first step from a laborer to the operator of various enterprises in Jerome, the Verde Valley, and California.

There were other saloons, too, but if one didn't advertise in the *Chronicle* he got scant mention, if any.

Mrs. Rudolph Rothermel ran the Cottage boarding house. Mrs. John H. (Kitty) Boyd ran the Boyd House, forerunner of the Boyd Hotel, now a Jerome landmark. The New Grandview Hotel occupied the site where the ruins of the Bartlett Hotel now rest; J. E. Meguire was the owner, and he was also Jerome's postmaster from 1893 to 1897.

Groceries and general merchandise were sold by T. F. Miller Company, Hull & Company, Doane and Horace Merrill and Con O'Keefe. Mrs. Keeler and Mrs. Alex Lyons had dressmaking establishments and Mrs. E. Trenberth was a milliner. J. H. Brown operated a barber shop, Allen Johnson was the town blacksmith, and Brisley & Tarr ran a drug store. Dr. Lee A. Hawkins had dental offices. Dr. Charles W. Wood was chief surgeon of the United Verde hospital, and Dr. M. A. Carrier had an independent practice. T. R. Brown managed the Jerome lumber yard. T. M. Cavenaugh operated the Jerome Livery and the Jerome Express. A branch of Prescott's Bank of Arizona was opened in 1899 and managed by Cashier Ralph A. Smith, with M. B. Hazeltine the nominal manager.

There were plenty of places to eat, both at the company boarding house and downtown. Chinaman Jim Sam had a restaurant; there was a Chinese restaurant in the Hull building, and there were others. There was a Chinese laundry. The *Chronicle* didn't think much of the Chinese, a feeling held by subsequent newspaper editors, with one exception, as related in a later chapter.

The *Chronicle* lasted only a few months. Later in 1895 William S. Adams started *The Arizona Mining News,* soon to become *The Jerome Mining News.*

The great fires of 1897, 1898, and 1899 altered the course of Jerome's history. The story of these appears in Chapter 11 of this book.

The nineteenth century closed on a wave of activity in the Black Hills. With the completion of the opera house which occupied the third floor of the Masonic or Miller building, troupes of performers gave the citizens a glimpse of what more populous cities enjoyed. The United Verde & Pacific railroad ran six trains a day. The great new Montana Hotel, the largest hostelry in the territory, it was claimed, was completed. A new four story, brick hospital had been built. A number of other mining properties were under development.

Angered that the Verde district was paying a large share of the county taxes and getting back less than a proportionate share for road building and other county services, citizens began agitating for a new county to encompass the Verde valley and environs. Clark County should be its name, *The Jerome Mining News* proclaimed. Clark weakly endorsed the idea of a new county but did nothing otherwise to promote the move for separation and the idea died for the time being, to be revived sporadically in later years.

In 1899 Jerome had a severe smallpox epidemic, resulting in a number of deaths. The Copper Company built for the town an isolated pest house, which was burned when the epidemic subsided. The papers made but scant mention of this.

Whenever occasions arose to inspire it, patriotism in Jerome ran high. It surged with the sinking of the Maine, and thirty young men of the town enlisted in the army. One, Oscar Wager, became one of Teddy Roosevelt's rough riders.

The winter of 1898-1899 brought to Jerome the severest weather it had ever experienced. Snow packed into icy trails; workmen on the way to the mine and smelter carried picks to chop footholds. While wagons from the valley struggled up the mountain road through the snow, produce being brought to market froze solid. Milk turned to ice in its containers. According to the *News,* milk was sold by the pound instead of by the quart and even whiskey froze in its bottles.

But such frosty spells seldom lasted long. The thawings which followed the freeze-ups were as bad as the ice and snow. They brought mud—a deep, thick, gummy adobe mud. It soiled clothing and would suck the shoes off one's feet. There was no paving in Jerome then and no sidewalks. On the most used paths and crossings boards would be laid to float pedestrians across. Frequently wagons mired down.

The summer of 1899 brought heavy rains, which contributed to one catastrophe with loss of life. The United Verde's brick assay office had been built over one of the mine's abandoned stopes. Rainwater penetrating the ground above caused the timbers of the stope to collapse, precipitating the building into the void. Three men were killed, two injured. One of those killed was a nephew of William A. Clark.

In 1899 the town council took a most important step—it contracted for the laying of water lines and the construction of storage tanks for its fire prevention system.

Jerome, circa 1880.

The New Century's First Decade

In the first decade of the twentieth century Jerome felt itself maturing. In 1900 the town had its first official head count as a political unit; Uncle Sam said the count was 2,861, but the boosters of the camp were sure a lot of people had been missed, and besides there were a lot of men and women scattered around the nearby hills.

In 1900 the population of the United States was 76,000,000, which grew to 92,000,000 in 1910. William McKinley was elected for a second term, then in 1902 was assassinated, bringing Theodore Roosevelt into the office. He was followed by Howard Taft in 1908. In this decade wireless telegraphy became of practical use, and Peary reached the North Pole. Carry Nation rampaged, and you could send a letter for two cents and a postal card for one cent. Jerome expanded rapidly after cleaning up the ashes of the big fires of the late nineties. It now called itself a city. Dissatisfied with the domination by the people on the Prescott side of the Black Hills in political and fiscal affairs, Jerome again began agitation for the division of the county. Tom Campbell when elected to the lower house of the territorial legislature pushed for the measure. Had he had real support from Senator Clark through his agent H. J. Allen, the effort no doubt would have been successful, but the contents of the money bags were being used to fight and defeat a measure to place a bullion tax on the products of Arizona's mines.

Jerome's citizens received a lift in spirit at the publicized claim that the United Verde had passed Michigan's famed Calumet & Hecla copper mines in production. The United Verde having gained national prominence, speculation regarding the wealth of William A. Clark, now a United States senator from Montana, became a popular journalistic game. One enthusiastic reporter, his pen dripping enthusiasm and awe, wrote in 1902 that new discoveries at the mine had increased the value of the property to two billion dollars and that Clark, naturally, had scorned an offer of two hundred million. The Senator, it was claimed, had become the richest man in the world, having surpassed in wealth such plutocrats as the Astors, the Vanderbilts, the Rockefellers, the Goulds, the Rothschilds, and all other men who had loomed large in the world of money. The name of Croesus as a symbol of vast wealth could be sneered at; beside Clark he would have been a poor man.

Jerome took it all in, and was proud. It was in that period that Jerome first came to be called "The Billion Dollar Copper Camp." Actually, it was half a century later before a billion dollars worth of metals had been taken from Jerome's Black Hills.

The first seven years of the decade brought one of the wettest periods in the history of Jerome. The perennial presence of mud never ceased to hamper and annoy. Every rain created morasses. In August 1902 a cloudburst flooded several smelter buildings, including the power house, causing the shut-down of the generator which supplied the town with electric current. The railroad passes were choked with debris. Residences were flooded when clogged drainage channels turned torrents of water into the residential sections of the town; in some cases rocks were washed into the houses along with mud. The Bitter Creek gulch below the smelter was filled with rocks and dirt to a depth of fifteen feet. The county road to the valley was washed out.

Disastrous precipitation continued through the winter of 1902-1903. A heavy snowfall in January caused the mine and smelter to shut down again. Melting snows brought more mud. But by March cleanups brought the smelter back into production, and again the workmen had pay checks and full dinner pails.

The following summer these experiences were repeated. The smelter was closed for several days after a July cloudburst. The railroad was blocked.

In January 1905 heavy rains practically isolated Jerome. The streets were bogs; the steeper sections of Main Street down to Walnut Gulch became gullies. Washouts occurred not only on Jerome's narrow gauge railroad but on the Santa Fe as well. Smelter production was slowed. Drainage into the upper levels of the mine caused a number of cave-ins, and a real disaster from another cause. Water seeping into one of the so-called fire stopes made contact with burning ores, creating a build-up of steam pressure; a concrete bulkhead which had sealed off the stope from working areas of the mine was blown out. The blast of hot steam and gases caught twelve miners, six of whom were killed, the others badly burned.

Down on the Verde record high waters caused floods and the loss of many acres of rich farm land.

Despite the weather, twenty-five new residences were built in 1906, and a new slaughter house was erected in Deception Gulch.

Heavy rains with their attendant miseries continued through the winter of 1907, but to balance things the year 1908 was a drought year and a shortage of water developed.

In the year 1907 a record was established at the United Verde mine, a bad one. In that year thirteen men were killed, making it the worst year ever experienced. A shocked city council decided that it must take a hand; they demanded a meeting with the United Verde officials and vigorously protested the slaughter. The officials assured the councilmen that they were taking and would continue to take all possible measures to promote safety, short of interfering with acts of God, such as the one responsible for the catastrophe in the fire stopes.

Genuine effort was made to provide for the workmen's safety, but it was ten years before a concentrated safety campaign was inaugurated.

Jerome had several severe epidemics to contend with in the first decade of the century. Smallpox invaded the town again in the fall and winter of 1901-1902. Again the Copper Company constructed an isolated pest house, and a man who had acquired immunity was hired to attend the patients at a premium wage—$5.00 a day. As always in such cases *The Jerome Mining News* was reluctant to publish details; it did not disclose the number of deaths during the epidemic. But the town had a good scare; public meetings were barred and schools and churches were closed. It was forty-five days before the pest house was vacated and burned.

Later the *News* published an article extolling the virtues of a new cure for smallpox discovered by Dr. Charles Wood, chief surgeon of the United Verde hospital and his assistant, Dr. L. P. Kaull. These doctors, it was disclosed, administered pure cider vinegar to the smallpox patients. Ten of those thus treated were able to leave their confinement within a month, and only a few of them died.

In 1903 Jerome had an epidemic of scarlet fever. Marshal Jim Roberts's family was hardest hit, his wife and four of his children having contracted the disease. Two of the children died.

Another scarlet fever epidemic, perhaps Jerome's worst, struck in 1907. A number of children died. The family which suffered the worst was that of Patrick F. Geary, a smelter foreman and one of the town's early pioneers. Of five children, all of whom contracted the disease, three died.

Scarlet fever invaded again in the fall of 1909, causing the closing of the schools for a month.

The town election of 1902 brought out a new party in opposition to the one already established, the Citizens'. Called the Labor party, it opposed the alleged domination of the United Verde in town affairs. They elected one candidate. The composition of the successive town councils during the three decades following incorporation is told in Section E of the Appendix.

In 1902 the first of many campaigns to raise money to drill for oil in the Verde Valley was begun. Over the years several so-called oil wells were drilled. All found water, some artesian, but no oil beyond possible traces.

As the fame of the United Verde expanded many journalists visited Jerome and wrote stories about it. They found little cooperation from the mine officials, for Senator Clark would permit but a minimum of information to be given out, especially of the underground mine. But the writers did have access to production statistics as published in the mining and financial journals, and from such data made rosy speculations as to what the United Verde was doing and what its future might be.

In 1903 Jerome loudly hailed the arrival of its first automobile, a Franklin purchased jointly by Walter Miller and Dr. L. A. Hawkins. When, despite predictions that no gasoline buggy could ever negotiate Jerome's steep grades, the car did prove its ability to travel around the valley, others were purchased. The camp was right up to date with telephone service, too—it had not only one, but two, 'phone companies in the early years of the decade. After a third company, the Overland, came in with long distance service in 1909, it absorbed the other two.

In 1904 Jim Roberts resigned as town marshal, and Fred Hawkins was appointed. Roberts was not to return to duty in the Verde Valley for twenty years.

In 1906, following the glad news that copper had risen to nineteen cents per pound, the United Verde announced plans to increase production to six million pounds monthly, a substantial increase over any production theretofore attained. In November the citizens were further cheered by the announcement that wages would be raised twenty-five cents a day.

In 1907 construction of the Hopewell tunnel was begun. It was driven eastward from the 1000 foot level of the mine. Excavation of this tunnel was started from each end simultaneously, and under the expert direction of chief mine engineer Clarence V. Hopkins a perfect juncture was made in September 1908, twenty-one months from its beginning. The tunnel was 6,600 feet long and exited on the hillside toward the river.

United Verde officials stated that the purpose of the Hopewell tunnel was to drain mine water and to dispose of waste from underground operations; but that it eventually was to be used for the transportation of ores became apparent a few years later when the company announced that a large new smelter would be built near the Verde river. Such a move was essential, as the Jerome smelter was constructed over mine workings, and settling ground continued to disturb the plant structures.

After the building surge which followed the big fires there was a decline of activities in the town, and the recession which occurred during the latter part of the period brought further decline. The census of 1910 showed a drop in population from the 2961 count of 1900 to 2393. As the price of copper declined the twenty-five cents per day increase which had been granted mine and smelter workers was withdrawn.

During the decade four of Jerome's best known men died. William Munds, Jerome's first mayor, died in 1903. In 1906 General R. H. G. Minty, one of the town's most famous citizens, passed away. In 1907 Captain John D. Boyd, an original locator of United Verde claims, died at Prescott. In 1910 Jerome's constable and deputy marshal Charles King was ambushed and brutally murdered.

Early day scenes on Jerome's Main Street. Above: Members of a lodge escort a deceased brother to the cemetery. Below: From horses to gasoline: Members of Jerome's Automobile Club line up for a holiday excursion.

The Second Decade

In the nation, President Woodrow Wilson followed Howard Taft as president in 1912; in that year too Arizona was admitted to statehood, and the nation was shocked at the sinking of the Titanic with the loss of 1500 lives. Francisco Villa raided into Texas and General Pershing invaded Mexico with orders to take Villa dead or alive. President Wilson was reelected, to lead the United States into the first world war.

George W. P. Hunt became Arizona state's first governor, with Jerome's Thomas E. Campbell the second. The "noble experiment" of prohibition got under way, and so did bootlegging.

Jerome grew rapidly on the heels of a mining boom. John Hudgens, who succeeded the murdered Charles King as deputy marshal, early proved to be a competent officer. An attempt to draw him into an ambush such as took the life of King ended in the death of his would-be assassin.

Its purchase of farm lands in the valley removed all doubt that the United Verde Copper Company was preparing to build a new smelter. In 1911 work was begun on the building of a broad gauge railroad from Cedar Glade on the Ash Fork to Phoenix line into the valley, its terminal to be a new community named Clarkdale in honor of the Senator.

In 1912 James S. Douglas and associates bought control of the United Verde Extension Mining Company and began the development which resulted in the discovery of bonanza ores in 1914 and 1915 and starting a mining boom. Worries over the effect the imminent abandonment of the Jerome smelter would have on the camp were dissipated.

In 1915 the new smelter at Clarkdale began producing copper. At Clemenceau the UVX started production in 1918.

The mining boom had elements of wildness. At the beginning of the decade eleven small mines were operating near Jerome; now there was a frantic scramble to file claims on any type of ground, without regard for mineral showings. All open ground for miles around Jerome was staked, even down to the boundaries of Clarkdale. Eventually about seventy-five so-called mining companies began to sell shares to a public all too eager to buy.

A list of Verde District mining companies will be found in section D of the appendix.

Because of increasing fear that German agents or sympathizers might sabotage the mine and smelter, home guard companies were formed both at Jerome and Clarkdale in 1917, and trained for action should events require. With the United States in the war, patriotic fervor was high. There were fifty-five volunteer enlistments from Jerome and vicinity, with many more to be drafted. WE ARE WITH YOU, UNCLE SAM! headlined *The Verde Copper News.* It was dangerous for anyone to insult the flag. For making obscene remarks about it one man was arrested and fined one hundred dollars. One man from Jerome and one from Clarkdale were taken into isolated spots in the valley and horsewhipped; one of them was plastered with gummy oil and feathers.

All of Jerome's liberty loan quotas were over-subscribed.

The arrival of labor organizers in the spring stimulated unrest among workmen at the mine, with threats of a strike.

In the fall of 1918 tragedy struck the Verde Valley when it fell victim to the so-called Spanish influenza which was sweeping much of the world. In Jerome it spread at an alarming rate. Public gatherings of any kind were immediately barred; schools, churches and theaters were closed. School houses and other available buildings were turned into hospitals. Doctors and nurses were enlisted wherever available, some with little experience, and volunteers were accepted whether trained or not. Among the physicians who helped out in the valley was Dr. Judd, Winnie Ruth's husband.

Jerome suffered at least seventy-five deaths from the disease; Clarkdale about twenty-five, and there were many more in other parts of the valley. Before the year's end the epidemic began to ease, though cases continued to appear well into the spring of 1919.

With houses built one directly below another on the steep hillsides, incidents occurred which, annoying to some, brought amusement to others. There were complaints that people on a higher level used the roofs of those living below for the dumping of garbage; "tossed salad," one wag had it. Boys, it was charged, had contests to see which of them was the most skillful in tossing pebbles into the chimneys of houses below. At least one complaint was taken to court; Joe Peila and wife sued the owners of the four story Jerome Hotel, alleging that the tenants threw refuse out of its back windows onto the roof of the Peila home directly below, and also spit tobacco juice down upon it.

In October of 1919 a motorcade from Jerome and Clarkdale made the rough run from the valley to the Grand Canyon to deliver the Verde district's greetings and a gift to King Albert of Belgium, hailed as one of the great heroes of the first world war. The king was accompanied by his queen and Crown Prince Leopold.

In 1920 Jerome was shaken by a scandal involving one of its police officers who was accused, with other prominent Jerome men, of criminal rape. Jail sentences resulted.

Mud on Jerome's streets was doomed. The town council voted a continuation of its paving program, bringing hard surfaces to those streets having the most traffic. By ordinance all property owners in the business district were required to build sidewalks in front of their establishments.

The women of Jerome joined the great army of those of the "gentler" sex who had won the right to vote, and they held their heads a little higher.

Of great importance to Jerome and the Verde valley was the completion in 1920 of the new highway from Jerome to Prescott across Mingus mountain.

In 1920's fall election John L. Sullivan of Jerome was elected county attorney, from which position he was to ascend to the office of attorney general of the state.

The year and the decade ended on a gloomy note, as copper prices were declining. A boomlet which had followed the ending of the war was over. The people of Jerome feared a shut-down of the mines and smelters of the district when the work force at the United Verde mine was reduced by two-thirds.

The United Verde Apartments, constructed in 1918, contained 33 units. (Jerome Historical Society, Bob Ross Col.)

The Third Decade

The post-war recession brought about the closing of Jerome's producing mines in 1921, starting the decade on a gloomy note; but a boom followed, then a collapse which came close to making of the Verde Valley a poverty-stricken area, a child of the great depression which started in 1929.

In 1920 the census takers counted 105,710,620 human beings in the United States, of which they credited 334,162 to Arizona and 4,030 to Jerome. Comparative figures for 1930 were 122,775,046, 435,572 and 4,932.

In this decade presidents of the United States were the unfortunate Warren G. Harding, silent Calvin Coolidge, and Herbert Hoover, whose administration had to bear the brunt of the stock market crash of 1929 and its aftermath. For governors Arizona had Thomas E. Campbell, George W. P. Hunt, and John C. Phillips.

Despite the shut-downs of 1921 Jerome showed no great despair, for it had experienced a number of such occurrences before, and never had it been so very long before the beneficent smelter smoke would again befog the town. The town council proceeded with plans to improve conditions. A paving program was completed and cement sidewalks were laid on streets which previously had no such conveniences. Even the outlying Hogback was to have sidewalks.

In midyear of 1922 the mines and smelters resumed operations. Work went on at the old smelter site in preparation for the open pit mining of ores.

In 1922 Lewis W. Douglas, who had joined the staff of the United Verde Extension Mining Company, was selected to the lower chamber of the state legislature, the beginning of a distinguished career in public service.

The next few years of Jerome's life were fairly quiet so far as municipal activities were concerned. But like the rest of the nation it became inoculated with the fever of speculation. There was a revival of trading in the shares of local mining properties. Almost everyone, from laborers to executives, bought stocks and went to bed at night with a euphoric glow and slept atop rosy dream clouds. The catastrophe of 1929 was the beginning of the saddest five years in Jerome's history.

The year 1924 was marred by another smallpox epidemic. It was one of Jerome's worst, with sixty cases and eleven deaths.

Early in the decade a great rivalry developed between Jerome and Clarkdale over sports, particularly baseball, which passed far beyond friendly status. The story of this and its aftermath appears in a subsequent chapter.

The year 1925 brought gloom to many Jerome citizens when the Bank of Jerome, with its parent, the Prescott State Bank, was closed by the state bank examiner. Paul H. Deming, the cashier, with assistant cashiers Ross and Earl Foreman, were indicted on a number of charges. After extensive trials all were released. The blow to depositors of the bank who were employees of the United Verde was softened by the generosity of the company in paying half their losses.

The Jerome branch of the Bank of Arizona of Prescott, under the guidance of M. B. Hazeltine, remained in sound condition.

Senator Clark died in 1925. The distribution of his estate among his sons and daughters opened the way for the contests which ended ten years later by the purchase of the United Verde assets by Phelps Dodge Corporation.

In 1928 Robert L. Finch was elected to the state legislature from the Verde Valley. He was employed as an accountant by the United Verde. Formerly of Tempe, he had already served three terms as a representative from Maricopa County. His namesake son in later years entered politics in California and subsequently became a member of President Nixon's cabinet.

The United Verde's big new hospital opened for service in 1922, but was soon found to be inadequate, and a fourth floor was added in 1929. It had a staff of fine doctors and nurses, and received patients from all parts of northern Arizona. This building, long vacant, is one of the landmarks of Jerome.

In 1929 the city demolished its old town hall and built a new hall and fire station. It is still in use.

Also in 1929 copper prices began to fall sharply, and continued to decline for four years. Production at the United Verde was cut

Above: The Jerome smelter in process of dismantling. Smoke from the new Clarkdale smelter shows in the distance. c. 1916.

Below: The same site after the big shovels went to work.

and many men laid off, with final and complete shutdown of the underground mine and smelter in 1931.

During the shutdown General Manager Robert E. Tally and President Charles W. Clark kept as many men at work as possible, largely on half time, with objections from some stockholders over the amount of money being spent. Employment was aided by a huge slide in the open pit which occurred in March 1931 and which deposited more than a million tons of rock on the pit's bottom, requiring a tremendous effort for its clearance. Also there was maintenance work to be done and a new shaft to be sunk. Employment was found for about two hundred men at Jerome; a skeleton crew was retained at the smelter.

The United Verde Extension after a six-months shutdown continued operations on a small scale. But with only a fraction of the payrolls that the town had been feeding upon Jerome was in for the harshest period, four years long, that it had ever known.

Welfare organizations were formed and aid was given to the most needy residents of the valley's various communities. Tons of carp were seined from Peck's Lake and distributed.

Thus Jerome managed to live on, feed its hungry, and hope for the day when smoke again would issue from the tall stacks in the valley. That day came when early in 1935 mining and smelting were resumed by the United Verde.

Quickly following came the startling news that the United Verde control had been taken over from the Clark family by Phelps Dodge Corporation. There were fears, especially among the supervisors, over what effect the change might have on their positions and their futures. But these fears subsided as they learned that the new managers were men of heart and integrity. Only a few were adversely affected by the change; many benefited, as Phelps Dodge's larger operations gave wider opportunities for enterprise and advancement.

It was in the third decade of the century that Nature assisted by man took a hand in shaping the physical aspect of Jerome.

In February 1928 a west coast newspaper printed a dispatch from Jerome in which it was predicted a horrible fate awaited the town. Following are some excerpts:

> Built over a great fault, this Arizona town of some 5,000 inhabitants is slowly slipping into the valleys surrounding the world's richest copper mine. . . .

Jerome is perched on the side of a huge ore-laden hill. . . . The business buildings and the workers' houses cling tenaciously to the slopes. . . .

Some time ago a pronounced slip was noticed. Crevices appeared in office buildings. Then a church fell down. The roof fell. The walls tumbled and the floor caved in. Fortunately no worshipers were caught in the crash. . . .

Visitors plainly see the jagged irregular cracks in the brick and concrete office structures, and the ominous bulges in walls and streets. . . .

Publicly geologists minimize the danger. . . . Secretly, however, they admit that the town is hopeless, and that some day the workers and business men must move to another hillside or down into the sheltered security of Deception Gulch.

Meanwhile, a slight earth tremor or a heavy fall of rain may bring on a catastrophe that could rock the world.

To that writer with his lugubrious prophecies a cause for wonder seemed to be that the Jerome natives "like the happy-hearted Italian villagers living near Vesuvius give scarcely a thought to the ever-present peril. . . . For, sooner or later, the yawning hole beneath will swallow up the town."

Though, as the citizens of Jerome well knew, Jerome was in no danger of a world-rocking catastrophe, what did happen was bad enough. A whole block of substantial business buildings on the east side of Main Street was demolished, as well as a sweep of buildings on Hull Avenue and eastward in what was the most populous section of Jerome. Down across Hull Avenue one can see, crowded with rubble in a stretch of barren waste, the remains of the reinforced concrete building which was once the town jail. It is some distance from its original site on the opposite side of the street. The tourist is invited to view this wreck as an indication of how a section of Jerome slid downhill—a section which included many stores, small hotels, lodging and boarding houses, and dwellings.

There was a considerable difference of opinion among engineers and geologists as to the exact causes of the ground movement which destroyed or damaged so many of Jerome's buildings, retaining walls, and streets. The following is an attempt to coordinate the various views into a probable sequence of causes.

The greater part of the divagating area was below an age-old fault which cut across the town above the business section. The disturbance caused by the original subsidence below the fault, later to be filled by the natural process of erosion from above, had created unstable ground without a normal bedrock underlay.

By the turn of the century the heavy sulphur fume from Clark's Jerome smelter and its contiguous ore roasting pyres effectively killed all vegetation in and around Jerome that had not been removed for use as mine timbers or fire wood. Without Nature's check to rapid run-offs, the drainage channels which had been built on the slope of Cleopatra Hill above the town, during hard rains at times were filled with rock and earth, causing excessive amounts of water to be discharged into the town. As the ground became waterlogged surface seepages appeared. Foundations were affected.

Mining was done by the United Verde Extension under a part of the subsidence area, and some claimed that caving in these workings contributed to the subsidence.

Then came the man-made earthquakes.

The layman may find it hard to imagine the vast quantities of explosives, many millions of pounds, used in excavating a hole in the ground such as the United Verde open pit. Thousands of vertical holes in the bed of the pit took from 50 to 5,000 pounds of powder each, usually a mixture of black quarry powder and dynamite. The shocks of all of these could be felt in downtown Jerome, but they were mild compared with detonations in the so-called tunnel blasts—the exploding of huge charges of powder set in tunnels driven in the walls of the pit. In six tunnels driven from 1924 to 1927, the smallest charge was 54,000 pounds; the last, the grand daddy of all such blasts up to that time, was exploded in a tunnel 110 feet long with cross-cuts at the end. The explosive charge was 260,000 pounds, the equivalent of six standard freight car loads. Windows rattled all the way to Camp Verde.

It would be fruitless to attempt to estimate the extent of damage contributed by each of the conditions and circumstances mentioned, but they all had some bearing. The United Verde Copper Company and the United Verde Extension Mining Company each acknowledged some responsibility, and jointly provided compensation in some degree to the owners of the buildings which had to be demolished.

Men of the Dinner Pail

Few communities anywhere depended so completely on the wages of the working man as the isolated mining camp.

Of this Jerome was a prize example. After the United Verde's second smelter began to pour copper in 1894, the town existed and grew almost entirely by benefit of the payrolls of the big mine and a few small mine operations.

In 1899 one of Jerome's newspapers boasted that the United Verde had a payroll of $50,000 a month. Though that estimate was probably low, such an amount seemed large in a day when roustabouts at the smelter received only $2.00 for a twelve hour shift, smeltermen $3.00 and miners $3.50.

People of the present day, accustomed to good pay and all the luxuries and benefits that result, find it hard to believe that men—and many of them with families—could exist on such wages. It is easier to understand when one considers that in those days T-bone steaks sold at fifteen cents a pound, stew meat at nine or ten cents, ground meat at seven cents, a pair of levis at seventy-five cents, and men's suits as low as five dollars. These were Jerome prices.

After the opening of the new smelter the working forces were gradually increased until, in 1900, the United Verde employed about 800 men. In 1902 the territorial legislature passed a law limiting underground workers to eight hours work a day. The Jerome smeltermen demanded equal treatment, but Senator Clark turned them down. A ten-hour day was conceded, but the workmen continued to insist that they too should have eight-hour shifts.

The mine and smelter men began a movement to organize a union. Clark opposed this, but not openly. There was unrest but no open rebellion until later in the year 1902 when smelter superintendent Tom Taylor laid off two of the furnace crew of thirty men. The men were not needed, he said. The other twenty-eight men struck in protest. General Superintendent Giroux ordered the men returned. This settled the disturbance for the moment, but dissatisfaction with wages, hours and working conditions continued among both the surface and underground men.

The grumbling continued on a rising scale then ceased abruptly when in the fall of 1902 Clark announced that mining and smelting would be discontinued for an indefinite period, the reason given being that there had been an over-production of copper. A few maintenance men would be retained; those laid off were advised to seek work elsewhere.

There was skepticism within and without the district as to the real reason for stopping the United Verde operation. Outside newspapers and journals speculated that the Jerome miners' union had become so strong that it was in a position to call a strike at any time, a condition the Senator would not tolerate. The shut-down and the laying off of men (including, of course, the potential troublemakers) was an effective way of squelching the union, it was suggested.

Severe damage caused by storms following the shut-down enabled quite a few of the unemployed miners and smeltermen to find temporary employment.

In December mining and smelting was resumed. The union spoke with a soft voice during the following year.

Early in 1904 the bricklayers made a demand for higher wages. Clark said no, claiming that there had been an agreement with the bricklayer's union that they were to work at less than the standard scale. If there had been such an agreement it was unilaterally dissolved by the bricklayers; they quit in a body and left the district.

Another example of the United Verde's method of settling strikes occurred in 1906, when furnace liners at the smelter threatened to strike unless their twelve-hour schedule was reduced to eight hours, without any reduction in their pay of $2.75 per day. Charles W. Clark, then general manager, again offered ten hours, but the liners refused this balm. Whereupon the announcement was made that the smelter would close down "for repairs and clean-up."

In November 1906 the general manager announced an increase of twenty-five cents per shift to all day's pay men, to continue while copper sold for over nineteen cents per pound.

By the end of 1906 the United Verde was employing more than 1000 men in its mines and smelter. Workers found it easy to find jobs in the Verde district. Aside from the big mine, much building was going on as increasing population pushed the camp's boundaries outward.

At the mine a cause for worry among the men was the high accident rate, due in part to the circumstance that trained miners were in scarce supply and the untrained men employed had not attained the schooling in their work and in safety methods necessary for the avoidance of accidents.

In 1907 Jerome was to have one of its periodic setbacks. High prices for copper had so stimulated production in the copper mines of the world that there was an over-supply and falling prices. The United Verde curtailed production by half, laid off men, and cut wages. Gradually normal production was restored, and there was little manifested discontent among the men of the working forces during the next few years.

In March, 1911, the company reduced the working hours of surface men to nine, but this did not satisfy the boilermakers, who demanded an eight-hour day. When this was refused they quit. The dispute threatened to spread to other labor classifications, whereupon the businessmen of the town decided to take a hand. They called a mass meeting in an effort to soothe the discontent. Under pressure of public opinion the boilermakers agreed to return to work on the same basis as before pending further consideration of their demands.

The legislature took care of the matter of laborers' hours at the new state's first session in 1912. A law was passed requiring that all workers in hazardous industries should be given an eight-hour day.

A new wage scale was negotiated with the Jerome miners' union, under which wage rates ran from $2.75 per day for car men and shovelers up to $5.25 per day for shift bosses. At the smelter wages were comparably adjusted but the men were paid by the hour—31 cents for roustabouts to 66 cents for shift bosses.

The activity engendered by the building of the new smelter and town at Clarkdale, starting in 1912, and the new railroads, involved a large force of men who didn't take the time to organize into unions; but after the Clarkdale smelter began producing copper in 1915, and Jerome discovered it didn't need a smelter to keep it alive and kicking, the work forces settled down and the unions, already established as satellites of the International Union of Mine, Mill and Smelter Workers, were greatly strengthened. New wage demands were formulated, and the growing threats of a strike came to a head on May 24, 1917, when the union called out its various units. The demands were, in the main, for higher wages, a closed shop, and check-off of union dues. The so-called Miami scale of wages was sought, that in force in the Globe-Miami district of Arizona. The wages paid were somewhat higher than in Jerome. All mines in the Verde District with operating crews of any size were affected by the strike. In addition to the United Verde and United Verde Extension, fourteen smaller mines were involved in shut-downs.

At the United Verde mining was not completely discontinued, as about 250 of the Mexican workers refused to join the strikers. Not many of the Mexicans were members of the striking union, having their own organization, Liga Protectora Latina.

Prominent among the Mexicans in helping to keep their fellow nationals on an even keel were Santiago Tisnado, Sixto Rodriguez, Cenobio Rivera, Carlos Miramon and Adolfo Pecina. Some of these served as deputy marshals during the war period.

The strike lasted only ten days. The Miami scale was granted, but not the closed shop and the check-off. Wages were to be on a sliding scale, based on the market price of copper. The settlement called for an immediate raise to $5.25 per day for miners and comparable classifications, with a base of $4.75.

The strike was marred by the tragic and useless slaying of two guards at the United Verde mine. Armed guards on patrol approached each other in the darkness at night, misunderstood signals, and a gun battle resulted.

Members of the Industrial Workers of the World—popularly known as "Wobblies"—had been gathering in Jerome, and they noisily attempted to insert themselves into the 1917 strike. The International Union denounced them as rabble-rousers dominated by the communists. When the strike was settled the IWW denounced the terms, and on July 6 called their own strike. Among their demands was a $6.00 a day wage for miners. The miners' union refused to recognize the Wobblies' picket lines, and in one case, armed with rocks and clubs, chased a group of pickets clear down into the town.

Active in the IWW strike was the notorious Micky Scanlon, chief agitator for Big Bill Haywood, head of the Wobblies.

MEN OF THE DINNER PAIL

Denouncing the IWW for its attempt to cause trouble after a settlement approved by a majority of the workmen had been reached were many of the residents of Jerome not associated with the mining companies. A group of them decided to do something about it. They did, and the story of their action literally sped around the world.

Following a secret meeting a group of more than two hundred Jerome citizens, on the morning of July 10, swarmed over and into every rooming house, den, flop joint, or other place where the Wobblies might bed down, and about a hundred men were rounded up. The IWW claimed a membership of 600 in the Jerome area, but a roster discovered during the roundup showed the names of less than a hundred men; so with the exception of a few who eluded the vigilantes and hastily departed under their own power the sweep was clean. A few of the men caught in the net were released at the request of mine supervisors who vouched for them, but seventy-five were loaded into box cars and sent away. A few escaped along the way; those remaining were released near Kingman, with orders not to return to Jerome. Only a few of them did at the time, but they began to trickle back, and early in 1919 there were about 150 in the camp.

Under the sliding scale agreement there had been some increases in wages, but a post-war lag in the market brought about the announcement early in February that the United Verde and the United Verde Extension would cut wages 75 cents a day. Cries of protest came from the workers; the IWW and some sympathizers, called by the copper companies "Sinn Fein agitators," announced they would call a strike. The companies countered by stating that should the disturbance not cease they would close their mines and smelters. The IWW did call a strike, and both companies promptly closed their operations. The shut-down was to be for three months or longer, it was announced.

It was in this period that Micky Scanlon, who had been active in the strike, entered suit against twenty-nine corporations, firms and individuals in Jerome, claiming that in the 1917 deportation the defendants "did seize . . . steal, take, arrest, and carry away the plaintiff," and "caused him to be herded in cars like *cattle.*" The suit died by the wayside.

The United Verde operation remained down until May; the United Verde Extension resumed in June.

But the demand for copper became weaker, and in 1921 both the big mining companies of Jerome closed down their mining and smelting. Out of a total force of about 2200 men the United Verde laid off all but 275. Of those retained married men were given the preference.

Both companies resumed operations in 1922.

During the balance of the third decade relations between labor and management remained on a fairly friendly footing. Wages continued to be regulated by the price of copper. At the United Verde a strong safety program was maintained. An extra-incentive wage or bonus system was placed in effect, under which workmen who were able to show greater efficiency than prescribed under standards set for each wage classification would receive extra pay.

Recreation facilities, as described elsewhere in this book, helped to keep employees contented.

This photo of a group of armed men in front of the T. F. Miller building was taken either during the May 1917 strike, or the Wobblies deportation.
(*Jerome Historical Society*)

11

FIRE! FIRE!!

That blaring headline appeared on the front page of *The Jerome Mining News* after the town's big fire of 1897, and editor Bill Adams bitterly remarked that he might well leave the type set up for the next big conflagration—for, as he had been telling the people all along, the town was just one big tinder box. He was right, too; he might as well have let the line stand. The citizens of Jerome knew of the potential danger, but they were too busy making money to take the time to organize for fire protection.

Mrs. Thomas, a colored lady from Phoenix who frequently visited mining camps as a representative of the Salvation Army, was talented in exhortation and claimed the gift of prophecy. After each of Jerome's big fires she proclaimed that God's hand held the torch that started each of the various holocausts, and that until this Sodom and Gomorrah, this sinkhole of corruption, this hag-ridden blight on the fair face of one of Arizona's beauty spots, repented and washed away its sins, Divine anger would not be dissipated and more fires would sear the slopes of Cleopatra Hill.

In the last years of the century outside newspapers began to refer to Jerome's conflagrations with such headlines as "JEROME BURNS —AGAIN!"

After the desolating fire of 1899 a Jerome newspaper reported, "five times the fire fiend has invaded Jerome." We know of four fires in the 1890's sufficiently devastating to be placed in the category of disaster. The first occurred in 1894; it ravaged a block or two in the business district of the town, the largest loss occurring from the destruction of merchandise and personal possessions, as the buildings were cheaply and flimsily built. We have more intimate details regarding the conflagrations of 1897, 1898 and 1899, each of which devastated the business district and consumed many residences and smaller structures.

The 1897 fire occurred on December 24 and brought a gloomy

Christmas to Jerome. *The Jerome Mining News* started its story of the event in this way:

> As Jerome was engaged in its Christmas eve pursuits, as the happy children were gleefully acclaiming their joys at Santa Claus in the Baptist Church, and the patients at the hospital were being given their nightly medication, the spirit of Christmas and good will prevalent throughout the camp, at the time above all others in the year, when peace, domesticity and comfort reigns supreme, the populace was startled by volley after volley of pistol shots. People ran excited into the open to see the sky illumined by forked tongues of flame.

Fortunately there was no wind that night, a blessing not bestowed on the town at succeeding fires. With such meager fire-fighting equipment as was at hand, mainly buckets and small hoses, the flames were confined to the business block north of the Fashion saloon. Twelve buildings were destroyed, including space occupied by four saloons and two restaurants, about the proportion indicated for Jerome's early days.

Dave Connor's building, on the site of the present Connor Hotel, was constructed of stone and was the only building in the block to escape total destruction. To the east of this building, in the short block along Jerome Avenue between Main Street and Hull Avenue, were four two-story frames. The one closest to Hull Avenue was occupied by an Oriental known as Japanese Charley; it was presumably a lodging house, but was actually a sporting house, with girls occupying the second floor. It was in this building that the fire started. An eyewitness account by Oscar Wager, as quoted by Roscoe Willson in a 1959 issue of *Arizona Days and Ways*, follows:

> My partner and I dropped into Connor's saloon for a drink, and on leaving were intrigued by a noisy quarrel in a Japanese sporting house in the rear of the saloon. Apparently some sort of a free-for-all was going on and we stopped and looked through a window. While we looked on, a woman picked up a kerosene lamp and threw it at a man. It missed the mark, but broke against the wall and almost instantly the interior of the flimsy building was a mass of flames. Everyone scrambled out of the inferno and then we heard someone say that one of the girls was lying dead drunk in a back room. My partner went in and carried her out and dumped her in the snow.
>
> By that time the whole front row was a roaring furnace, and the town

had practically no fire protection. The flames spread so rapidly through the business section that there was almost no time to save the goods. The saloon keepers hollered "Come and get it! All the whiskey you want for carrying it away!" A good many irresponsible people desisted from fire fighting, sacked the saloons of all they could carry, and guzzled whiskey while the major portion of Jerome's business district burned to the ground.

Another rescue that found space in the News was accomplished by Dan Slaughter, a Negro in the employ of Dr. Charles Woods. A girl named Charlotte rented rooms above Alex Cordiner's Peerless Saloon in the Roberts Block next to Japanese Charley—the second building to burn. Charlotte was surrounded by flames when Slaughter bounded up the stairs, threw a blanket around her, and carried her to safety.

Another lady to lose her all was Jennie, a well known madam of the town often referred to in the papers in a tongue-in-cheek manner. She occupied apartments in her own building on Main Street north of the Connor building, a section referred to in the News as "the Tenderloin district." Jennie claimed the greatest loss of all the property owners, $5500, of which $4000 was the value of clothing and jewelry.

Fortunately the fire did not travel southward or up the hill. The company hospital across the street from Main Street was endangered but saved by United Verde employees who were able to garner enough water from the overcrowded main to drench the face of it.

The ashes had hardly cooled before men were hard at work rebuilding. There was talk of incorporating the town in order that money might be raised for providing better fire protection, but the larger property owners, led by George Hull, argued so strongly against it that the movement died. They wanted no additional taxes.

The new buildings were soon completed and occupied, most of them as flimsy and inflammable as before. The resinous smell of newly sawn lumber still scented the air when, according to Mrs. Thomas, by Divine decree Jerome was sentenced to endure another conflagration, the worst Jerome was ever to suffer.

The date was September 11, 1898.

Each of the previous fires had been called "the big fire" in its turn, but by comparison with this one the earlier burns were small. It was worthy of the designation "big," as it ate up all of the town's business area and more than half of the residence and smaller structures. Included in the destruction was the plant of *The Jerome Mining News,* so we do not have the benefit of a local story from the pen of Bill Adams. We rely on the accounts of old timers, and details of the fire and its aftermath related by H. J. Allen in correspondence with William A. Clark. Passages from this correspondence follow:

> The entire town was wiped out by fire this morning, including all of the company dwellings east of General Minty's house with the exception of one cottage. The hospital is also gone. The Masonic hall, where the iron work is up three stories, came out of the flames in fair shape, only a few of the I-beams being warped and the masonry and brick-work seeming to be practically uninjured. The fire caught the Baptist church, but was extinguished, and the blowing up of two small cottages just opposite of that point is what saved the rest of the hillside and possibly Miller's store. There are about twenty-one houses left on the hillside, company dwellings and Miller's store.
>
> The fire started at about 7:15 this morning at the extreme north end of Hull Avenue, and was caused by a drunken Austrian, so the story goes, attempting to kindle a fire with kerosene. At 9:30 the entire site of the stores was waste. The works were shut down at the alarm and our men fought fire as well as they could with insufficient water supply, and with dynamite and giant powder. . . .
>
> The house where I was living was destroyed. All the furniture with a quantity of other effects was lost. My team was saved from the livery, and I drove Mrs. Allen and the children to the Cottonwoods, where we are pleasantly situated.
>
> A recent arrival named Rushmore, an undertaker, was found dead under one of the houses blown up by dynamite. Patients in the hospital were moved to the Baptist church. The school house was thrown open to the homeless, also private homes which escaped the fire. The company employees organized a relief committee to look after any cases of suffering. Miller ordered one hundred tents by express to take care of those not accomodated. There are enough provisions to last the population three or four days, with more goods coming from Prescott and Phoenix. Prescott and other places offered assistance, but all offers were declined. To stop petty stealing a safety committee of twenty men was sworn in as deputy constables. No liquor was to be had after the fire except what was sold by the saloon up at the Bend, run by a man by the name of Shea.

Mrs. Iva Carrier Shaw, daughter of Dr. Myron A. Carrier of early-day Jerome and the valley, furnished this writer an eye-witness account of the fire. She stated that the devastation progressed down Main Street east as far as the Hogback, and south on School Street nearly to the school house.

In a later communication to Clark, Allen reported that the damage to the Masonic Hall building was much greater than at first suspected, much of the iron being burned out and the masonry badly cracked.

The citizens of Prescott were stirred by the ill fortune of their neighbor, held a mass meeting, and raised a considerable sum of money. A committee of sympathizers brought the money to Jerome. Allen, who had assumed charge of all relief work, told the committee that outside help was not wanted and the contribution was refused. This rejection of aid offered in a generous spirit caused some resentment.

This action on Allen's part illustrates the policy of Clark to resist interference by outside sources in the affairs of a community which he considered his own domain.

Many of the United Verde employees whose homes or lodgings had been burned out drew their pay and left the camp. The mine and smelter operations were slowed by the loss of these workers.

Jerome quickly became a town of canvas, tents being placed in any convenient spot, even in the streets. An accompanying photograph shows the appearance of the town, the tents plainly showing.

On the day of the fire a separate blaze destroyed one of the principal bridges on the narrow gauge railroad, interrupting all freight service except for that material which was light enough to be conveyed by manpower across the gulch the bridge had spanned. Passengers had to traverse the gulch to board a train sent from Jerome.

An actual count of the number of structures consumed is not found, but about thirty business houses, about the same number of company dwellings, and about half of all other residences in the town were lost.

The woeful lack of an adequate supply of water and fire fighting equipment was again so strongly emphasized that the solid citizens of the town with but few exceptions decided there should be no further delay in taking steps necessary to provide protection. To raise the needed money incorporation was required, and a majority of the property owners in a thirty-five acre tract which included the business district and many of the residences petitioned the board of supervisors

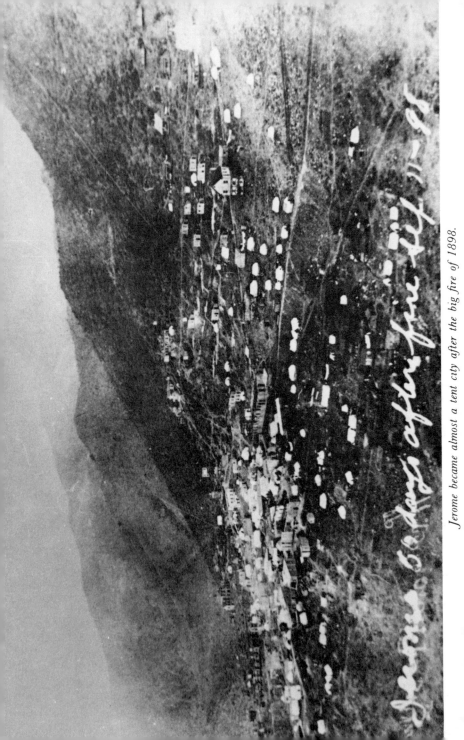

Jerome became almost a tent city after the big fire of 1898.

of Yavapai County to grant incorporation. Early in 1899 the supervisors voted incorporation for Jerome.

There was some resistance. George W. Hull, the largest land owner in the town, fought the move on the basis that it would result in burdensome taxes. Also, his own influence in the community would be curtailed. H. J. Allen was cold toward the movement, for he wanted no authority or influence other than his own in the management of the town.

The new council promptly outlined a fire district and adopted a building code designed to lessen the occurrence of fire. The code didn't go very far; its main provision was to compel the construction of stone or brick chimneys in new buildings.

While there was as yet no restriction on the use of wood in the rebuilding of the town's business houses, a number of the businessmen did take precautions. Some concrete fire walls between buildings were constructed. Dave Connor built a substantial two story hotel of brick—it still stands. The new company hospital was of brick and stone. Hoover and Cordiner employed a Los Angeles architect to design a new building for their Fashion Saloon, to be of reinforced concrete and "absolutely fireproof." Other builders were using brick for their new business places. A brick yard at Jerome Junction was kept operating at full blast.

Madam Jennie was in such a hurry to get her new "lodging house" in operation that she ignored the safety factor and put up another frame building. The town came close to suffering another disaster in April when a fire developed in this building, but it was extinguished before it could spread. Taking note of this Bill Adams asked editorially:

> Must it take another fire to convince the citizens that we must have more water to protect our city? Yet there are those trying to annul our incorporation and prevent action by the city to improve fire protection.

Adams referred to an action which Hull had started in an attempt to have the incorporation annulled. Hull's attorneys he branded as "shysters." Hull's suit failed in the county superior court, and the territorial supreme court upheld the judgment.

Yes, it did take another fire to stir the town council and other Jerome citizens to more energetic action. On May 19, 1899, disaster struck again—the third time in seventeen months. Extracts from *The Jerome Mining News*'s account of the fire follow:

Friday proved that every man and woman, and every child in Jerome, is a prophet. They had all prophesied for months that fire would come again and wipe out the town, and their predictions came true.

A few minutes after ten o'clock on the morning of Friday, May 19, the town was startled by the cry of "Fire!" It was quickly located in the Leland Hotel, a large two-story frame building on First Street between Main and Hull Avenue and east of the Kuchler-Munds-Bradley block. When discovered the fire had reached such headway that it was an impossibility, with the heavy wind from the south to assist it, and no water to extinguish it, to confine it to the neighborhood in which it had started, so every effort was made to save all property possible in the buildings north of the fire.

The pine, cloth and paper buildings which had been hurriedly erected after the fire of September 11th of last year made splendid fuel for the flames to devour and in a few minutes they were eating their way through the north of town with wonderful rapidity.

From the Leland to the Ryan Hotel on the east and the bowling alley on the north, and east to the brow of the hill, the flames spread, licking up everything in their way until they reached the residence of Dr. Carrier, where it stopped; north through Grand View block to the Hoover and Cordiner fireproof building, thence northeast to the frame buildings east of the Hoover and Cordiner building; east to and through Chinatown; back west to the Hotel Connor and then north to opposite the company's new hospital.

The heavy south wind prevented the spread of the flames in that direction. Where the flame could reach inflammable material it did its work well, and the only portions of buildings of any kind left standing in the burned district are the walls of the Hoover and Cordiner cement building, the brick walls of the Hotel Connor, the adobe walls of the C. M. Clark building, the brick Masonic hall and the brick block of Kuchler, Munds and Bradley.

Dr. Cody, who had an office in the Leland Hotel, was perhaps the first person to discover the fire, which started in the office of the hotel, but it was then burning so fiercely that, although he made heroic efforts to extinguish it, during which time he received some very severe burns about the face and hands, he was driven from the room by flames, and rushing downstairs grabbed a few of his instruments and was compelled to beat a hasty retreat to the rear of the building, the front being a mass of flames.

The article stated further that thirty businesses were burned out, together with forty dwellings south of Main Street and down the hill in the Mexican quarter. The area called Chinatown was to the north of the Mexican section.

The Hoover and Cordiner building (the Fashion Saloon) was held up as an example of what fireproof construction could mean to the business district. This despite the fact that the interior was completely burned out. That it was burned out was blamed on the circumstance that the fireproof doors and the metal shutters for the windows had not yet been hung. The owners were just ready to open for business; the basement was crammed with furniture and liquor. When these contents caught fire the flames ate away the wooden girders supporting the concrete roof, which collapsed. But the remaining shell of the building was solid, and the interior and roof were soon restored. It has withstood more than seventy years of weathering and shifting ground, and today houses the mine museum of the Jerome Historical Society.

The interior of the Connor Hotel across the street was also completely gutted, but the brick walls stood and stand today.

"Before the ground was cool," the *News* stated, "teams were at work removing the rubble from the burnt district and were digging for foundations for new fireproof buildings." Most of the businessmen were able to find the money to rebuild, but a few, after three catastrophes, found themselves with no assets and were forced to quit. Some didn't even have tents to fold before they stole away.

After the fire assistant postmaster Tom Campbell sold stamps from a cigar box and distributed mail on the street.

Hoover and Cordiner set up a bar in the basement of their Fashion Saloon building within a few days. Others sold merchandise from makeshift stands.

The town council acted promptly with stiff building and fire codes. No more tents and canvas covered shacks could be built anywhere within the town limits. Those already built must be removed immediately; if the owners would not act the town marshal would. The area in which fire resistant buildings must be built was extended. Plans were made to raise money by a bond issue for new high pressure water lines, hydrants and tanks, which were duly installed. Fire companies were formed, and trained in the manipulation of their new hose and hose carts; enthusiasm was maintained by frequent contests between the teams.

One indefatigable business person who refused to quit after the third burning was the subject of the following news item:

"Jennie is still on deck and will be doing business at the old stand with a fireproof building in a few days."

Another unquenchable lady, previously mentioned in this chapter, got publicity in *The Arizona Republican* of Phoenix in the following article under the heading "CLAIMS GOD DID IT:"

> There were many wild rumors in Phoenix yesterday when the first incomplete news of the Jerome fire reached town. There was one man here who was present at the destruction of the camp last September. Mrs. Thomas, one of the representatives of the Salvation Army, was there at the same time. She was using the fire as an object lesson, a visitation of God's wrath upon the sinful camp. She stood in the street and prayed for the Sodom and Gomorrah of Arizona, and said she was pained to see that the fire had not purified the place. She predicted that God wasn't done with Jerome yet. Since He had commenced He would regenerate the town or He would have no town there.
>
> Her auditor met her on the street yesterday and said, "Well, I see you have prophesied straight. God has taken another fall out of Jerome."
>
> "Yes," replied Mrs. Thomas, with the pardonable satisfaction of one who is on the inside, "God isn't going to give up the fight with Jerome. He'll burn it down a dozen times, as fast as they could build it up. He's started in to make Jerome a Christian town and it'll be Christian or nothing. Jerome might as well give up first as last and save money."

Shortly after that Jerome acquired two more churches. Perhaps that helped God to take pity on the satan-ridden town, for while Jerome was not through with fires there were no more of like proportions to shock this mountain community.

These are some of the fires that occurred in later years:

In 1902 four houses burned on the Hogback, not then reached by fire lines.

In 1907 eight buildings in the foreign quarter were consumed.

In 1911 a group of four houses on School Street were lost. In the same year T. F. Miller Company's warehouse burned, together with

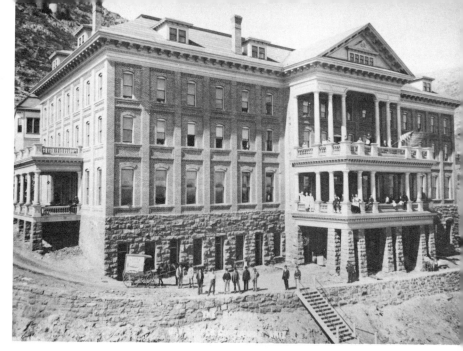

"The finest and most ornate hostelry in Arizona Territory," Senator Clark's *Montana Hotel. Above: As it appeared upon its completion in 1900. Below: Fifteen years later.*

their stables. Vehicles, eight mules, and five horses were incinerated.

In 1915 the big Montana Hotel, pride of Jerome, was completely gutted.

A bad fire occurred in the foreign quarter in 1917, and only the fact that Jerome then had an efficient mechanized fire department kept the business district from being destroyed again. An entire block was burned, including rooming houses, dwellings, and other structures. About ninety families, five hundred people, were made homeless.

A fire even more severe occurred in the same quarter in 1918. Sixty buildings were lost, rendering one thousand people homeless.

In 1926 a fire in the gulch below the Jerome Hotel destroyed two large rooming houses and fifteen small residences. A man and a woman were burned to death.

In 1927 seven houses were burned and four others damaged in the gulch below the Hampton House—the second United Verde hospital remodeled into a lodging house. Uptown a bakery and an apartment house were destroyed and a dry goods store damaged.

And so it went. Had Mrs. Thomas been around undoubtedly she would have declared that God was still dissatisifed with Jerome, Arizona's Sodom and Gomorrah.

Though not of the town, another fire, of long standing and costly, may be mentioned. It was the fire in the sulphide ore masses in the United Verde's underground mine. All attempts to extinguish it failed until it was attacked from above through the open pit. The burning ore was shoveled out.

Fire in the foreign district, 1917. (Jerome Historical Society)

That Wicked City

Early in the twentieth century, after the Jerome community had developed to the point where visitors had opportunity to consider the character of the town as separate from the bonanza mine, many articles appeared in the country's newspapers and magazines relating to the camp, and some of the writers in agreement with Mrs. Thomas began to characterize Jerome as being depraved and iniquitous, elaborating and extending admissions made in some quarters locally.

Some of Jerome's citizens seemed rather proud that their town had surpassed the reputation of places like Tombstone, but not Bill Adams of the Jerome Mining News. He was ready at the drop of a quad to tie into anyone maligning his fair city. He seemed to find merit in the fact that in this camp of 2500 inhabitants there were only twelve saloons (the limit by town ordinance), whereas towns that were *really* wicked had by tradition at least one saloon to every hundred denizens. Quoted below is one article that aroused Adams's ire; it appeared in *The New York Sun* as a despatch from Jerome dated February 5, 1903. Headlines are included.

THIS JEROME IS A BAD ONE—THE ARIZONA COPPER CAMP NOW THE WICKEDEST TOWN
It has Succeeded to the Place Held by Abilene and Other Frontier Towns—Dance Halls and Gambling Saloons Wide Open—Little Bloodshed

Jerome, Ariz. Feb. 5—Thirty years ago Bodie, California, with its daily murder and periodical lynching, was called the wickedest town in America. Then the rise of the cattle industry and the development of cowboys on the plains gave the palm for general cussedness to Dodge City and Abilene, in Kansas; Denison, Texas, and Julesburg, Colorado were famous for awhile for their depravity. Next there was Tombstone, Arizona, with its 164 saloons and dozens of gambling halls, in a population of 6,000. Wild Deadwood, in the Black Hills, and bad Leadville, Colorado, were known far and near as the wickedest towns during the 80's. Ten years later the title passed to Cripple Creek and Creed, Colorado.

Nowadays there is no dispute, in the Southwest, at least, that this copper camp of Jerome is the wickedest town in America. It has been purged with fire three times, and some people think it needs a fourth purging.

There is scarcely a more strangely situated town in the country than Jerome. Long before the traveler on the crookedest railroad on the continent reaches its eastern terminus, the town of Jerome may be seen "plastered," as it were, against the eastern slope of a bleak and desolate mountain. As the railroad train twists among the sunbaked foothills, one has an almost constant view of Jerome from the car windows.

A gray cloud of sulphurous fumes always hangs over the town. Away above the cloud, some 7,000 feet, one may see the peaks of the mountains. Some 5,000 feet below, at the foot of the mountain range is the Rio Verde, which foams and fusses on its way among the rocks and crags to the Salt River, 150 miles to the south.

From any vantage spot in Jerome one may look to the horizon in any direction, and an immense landscape of desolate mountains, rising one above another, chains of brown hills, sterile valleys, stupendous crags and a measureless area of dun and yellow desert wastes meets the eye. As far as the eye may range not a green thing in nature may be seen.

Yet there is scarcely anywhere a community where the per capita income is larger than at Jerome. Some eight hundred men are employed in the United Verde mines and in the enormous copper smelters. The weekly payroll ranges up to $50,000, and 80 percent of it is quickly spent in the little town.

The streets of Jerome run up and down the steep mountain. While there are a few neat, homelike cottages at the upper end of Main Street, the town is largely made up of primitive, rough board structures, houses with canvas sides and shingle roofs and cloth partitions. There are a few well-built stores and lodging houses.

Along the east side of Main Street there was until the recent fire a row of big hemlock and pine buildings interspersed with tents with board floors, and here were pioneer stores, saloons, dance halls, Chinese restaurants, lottery houses and wash houses.

"Up here," said a man, waving his hand toward the cottages scattered over the bleak upper mountains, "is where decent folks live; but down there on Main Street is where other folks live at night and where the money's made; oh, this is the hottest camp in the territory."

The blowing of the steam whistle at the United Verde mines marks the beginning of each chapter in the life of Jerome. Presently squads

Above: Jerome viewed from the Gulch, circa 1920. (Jerome Historical Society)
Below: Jerome foreign district and part of the business area, circa 1910.
(Jerome Historical Society, G. M. Sharp Col.)

of stalwart men come out of the mining tunnels and up from the shafts, and, coats on arm and dinner pail in hand, hasten for home and lodging houses, while a small army of grimy faced men issue from the smelters. The narrow streets which climb up and down the mountain side are congested with noisy miners and all the eating houses are thronged with hungry patrons.

By the time the lamps are lighted and the moon is rising over the San Francisco peaks the new chapter in the life of Jerome is under way. The night shift of bartenders and gamblers in the saloons have come on duty, the dancing women are decked in their most fetching finery, the paid musicians have warmed up and the storekeepers are ready for business. The saloons are crowded by men and women by eight o'clock. The faro dealers have got out their stacks of chips and coin and have seated themselves for the night; the poker men have their tables ready for the players, the roulette croupiers are turning the wheel and calling to people to come and woo the Goddess Fortune, and the craps men are demonstratively throwing the dice and noisily announcing the results of each throw.

The banjo, accordian, piano and violin players are in their places, ready for the nightly round of music. The young women who are hired to keep up the bar receipts are making friends with the men who have money and like strong drink.

The mining camp of Jerome is wide awake. From sunset to sunrise the seamy side of Jerome booms. The thoroughfares are alive with men from early evening until midnight. The dance hall herders keep the floors of the halls alive with men and women dancers and the bartenders lose no chance to sell drinks to anyone.

Every night there is a drunken row of some sort. Gambling, drink and women cause just such occurrences. Once in a while the brawl results in a pistol shot and stabbing, but this is only occasional, for Jerome, with all its wild ways, is singularly free from bloodshed.

With the earliest tinting of the sky over the mountain peaks to the east there comes a rapid decline in the night's revelry. The saloons and dives empty of the men and women who have lingered there. The professional gamblers cash up their chips, fill their canvas sacks and quit. The night shift of bartenders count their cash and make ready to turn the money and bar to the day shift.

Presently the stores reopen, and the sweepers and furbishers of the saloons come sleepily forth. An army of men come down the hillside from the mines and smelters. The 7 o'clock whistle blows and sober men are once more at their toil. The night in Jerome has passed away like an ugly dream.

THAT WICKED CITY

When Editor Adams printed the foregoing article in his newspaper, he introduced it with the following headlines and comments:

A DESCRIPTION OF JEROME BY THE NEW YORK SUN
Its Representative Smokes Too Much "Hop," and Under Its Influence Writes a Most Ridiculous and Slanderous Article About One of the Most Law Abiding Cities in America

The News has received from New York a Valentine, with the compliments of the editor of the New York Banker tacked thereto. The valentine is a word picture of the City of Jerome as seen by a *NEW YORK SUN* representative, who, when he, she, or it penned it, must have been under the influence of some drug, for not even the rankest of tanglefoot could create as disturbed a brain as concocted such an article as the *Sun* printed.

If the writer had been in his right mind he would not have had the moon rise in the north, and built imaginary dance halls, something Jerome has never had. Sulphur smoke is something all the inhabitants have been praying for for months. [The mine and smelter had been shut down for several months and had just reopened when this was written.] Saloons she has but twelve; one justice of the peace who does not have three prisoners before him each week of the year, one night and one day officer. . . . the *Sun's* article doesn't call for much comment.

Adams appended a final comment: "If you see it in *The SUN* it is not so."

A letter to a Phoenix newspaper by a Jerome correspondent written three and a half years earlier helped pave the way for other screeds branding Jerome as a wicked city. At this point in the publicity Adams' comments inferred ridicule rather than ire. This letter with headlines appears below. The explanation for the reference to the governor is that in 1899 the territory's chief executive N. O. Murphy had stirred up a storm in Jerome by indicating that some of the Verde District mining operations were really wildcat promotions.

TERRIBLY CENSORED (sic) JEROME
The Outside World Don't Know a Thing
About Her

The following letter appeared in *The Phoenix Enterprise* and will be read with much amusement by this, the second greatest mining camp in Arizona:

Jerome, Arizona, August 26 [1899]—The daily papers of Phoenix with one exception [*The Enterprise*] are now devoting considerable space to this lively mining camp. They seem to be advocates of Governor Murphy, an official who has made himself most obnoxious to the mining interests of this section. Contributions to the Phoenix press have been made to appear to reflect Jerome's sentiment and have placed the Jerome public in the wrong light. The blacklisted properties are being developed at the rate of three shifts every twenty-four hours, with no sign of abatement.

The petition to remove the governor is considered a timely rebuke to an unnatural official. The local papers are clear of mentioning anything that occurs hereabouts likely to ruffle the self-satisfied Jeromeites. In fact, it is said that some of the newspaper men were imported from a distance to conduct a paper to voice the sentiments of the owner of the new legislature. It has taken armed men to protect the plant of this publication during a political campaign, yet there has not been one word of the true state of affairs permitted to reach the outside world. Talk about the Inquisition! Spain can learn points from the Jerome council. The jail is quite near the palatial residence of the mayor of the town, and to prevent noisy drunken men from disturbing his honor's sweet repose, a cell has been prepared to sober them. The room is 6 x 7 feet, without ventilation. The floor is thickly studded with sharpened spikes; a small square in the center is left free from them. Here the poor drunken wretch must stand upright; if he jumps about he must hit the bull's eye or light on the spikes. Probably there is not such a town in the country, and nowhere else is the halcyon days of the great mining towns of Virginia City, Cripple Creek and Leadville carried to such lengths as here.

The Chinese play undisturbed all their national games. The big saloons are crowded day and night by gamesters. Payday the town is visited by gamblers from all parts of the territory, who stay until the play drags. Gambling is epidemic. The people will bet on anything. The newsboys flip a nickel with their customers to ascertain if they pay ten cents or nothing for a paper. The ladies turn their literary societies into card clubs. Jerome is not a city of churches, but hopes "to be worse by and by." As the cream of her society has organized a game run strictly on gambling principles, the poor tinhorn gambler is asking the question, Why should he pay a license and the rich play high five and rake in a benefit at the end of the quarter without paying? There exists a club in this town of sulphur and smoke which meets weekly and consists of 36 members; each gives a dollar each quarter as fees, the fund to be used to purchase some article to be striven for by the gaming club, who represents some of Jerome's so-called best citizens, counting among their number a councilman. The rustle of silk and the flash of diamonds form a part of its make-up. It is true you fail to hear the coarse jokes and loud exclamations which accompany the crap table, but gambling is gambling, whether it is a kid-gloved affair, or the darkey making a shot at the table of his choice—craps. While one of the town's boasted editors devotes almost a column of his paper in criticizing the struggling minister of one poor little church for the way he asks for barely enough to keep body and soul together, verily a Sodom and Gomorrah case.

Note: The statement regarding "the owner of the new legislature" refers to William A. Clark, who through his agent H. J. Allen was said to dominate the territorial legislature.

It is true that there had been a spiked cell in the town jail, though it was seldom used. Probably due to the unfavorable publicity it was done away with.

In reminiscences published in *The Verde Copper News* in 1920, J. A. Thompson admitted to having published in *The Jerome Reporter* during a political campaign some violence-breeding material that led him to employ armed guards for the protection of himself, his brother, and his plant.

The Fashion Saloon, located on the corner of Main Street and Jerome Avenue. (Jerome Historical Society)

Flags and logos of Jerome's news media from the first to the last.

13

Jerome's Fourth Estate

Among the world's greatest optimists surely must have been the pioneer newspaper man—the printer or the reporter whose blood ran hot with the urge to publish his very own sheet. In 1900 Jerome harbored only 2861 people, according to the census takers, a considerable percentage of whom could neither read nor write the English language; yet in that year three weekly newspapers were being published in the camp and having a merry time fighting each other. Five years prior to 1900 another weekly had been born, but it had died in infancy.

Almost every active mining camp had at least one newspaper in its early life. Presses came by ox or mule team, and the papers printed might grow if the camp grew, or abruptly expire if the camp declined—or the publisher accumulated too many debts or enemies.

The smell of printer's ink seemed to act upon the hopeful editor's senses both as a stimulant and as an opiate. It aroused the feeling that the pen, his pen, was mighty, and at the same time dulled his ability accurately to assess his chances for survival. One newspaper would have been enough in Jerome at any time; with three the situation was ripe for battles. The conflicts were mostly verbal; apparently only one editor lost any blood, and that without the prestige a gun fight would have created.

The first Jerome newspaper was established in 1895, shortly after Clark's new smelter was blown in. Named *The Jerome Chronicle,* its founder was Herbert Eugene Wilcox. He came to the camp from Globe, Arizona, home of the Old Dominion mine, where he had been employed by the Globe Silver Belt newspaper. He was intrigued by the many press reports relating to the great bonanza in the Black Hills owned by a Montana millionaire.

Wilcox's evaluation of Jerome as a fertile field for an independent newspaper proved faulty. His journal would be independent, he announced editorially, and he set out to prove it. He recognized capital, but principally as sustenance for labor, a policy not in line with that of the Copper Company as represented by H. J. Allen. Wilcox was to learn that Allen was a real power not only locally but in the county and state; it was said that he held the territorial legislature in one hand while he fed it from a money bag in the other. When Wilcox called on him he was received coldly.

"We neither need nor want a newspaper in Jerome," Allen declared. "You cannot make one pay."

Wilcox was determined to prove Allen wrong. The first issue of *The Jerome Chronicle* appeared under date of March 2, 1895. It was a four page, seven column sheet, to be issued weekly.

In outlining the paper's policy, Wilcox editorialized that in addition to being independent and conservative he would work for statehood for Arizona; to bring the territorial prison from Yuma to the Verde Valley; and to make Jerome a twin sister of Butte, Montana. The *Chronicle,* Wilcox said, recognized no class, click (sic) nor creed. He greeted the stockmen and farmers in the firtle (sic) valley of the Verde, and pledged to do all possible for their prosperity and happiness.

Wilcox had asked Allen for information regarding the United Verde's mines and smelting plant that he might publish in his paper. He was given none. But from undisclosed sources he obtained enough information to provide material for several articles descriptive of the United Verde properties and operation. Allen was angry; such publicity was something that he, charged with holding down property valuations and taxes and killing legislation unfavorable to the mines, definitely did not want.

About twenty of Jerome's business houses and professional men and women took limited advertising space in the *Chronicle,* including the most prominent of the saloons, but absent was anything at all from the United Verde Copper Company and the T. F. Miller Company, the "company store" owned by William A. Clark and relatives.

As in Jerome newspapers to follow, in the early issues of the *Chronicle* crime in the camp was played down. The outside world must believe that Jerome was a pure and peaceful mining community, a place for quiet family living. Here is a prime example of such evasion:

"There was a stabbing affair a few days ago. So humiliating to a lawabiding citizen that the less said about it the better."

There weren't many personals in the *Chronicle.* There were a number of references to "fistabouts," deplored, but with the names of the participants withheld. But in the thirteenth issue, with the paper then on the financial reefs, Wilcox abandoned such prudery, and went all out in describing a murder and its aftermath. After Charles Ward, a well known Verde District mining man, had beaten Jake Brown over the head with a cane Brown shot him. Ward lingered awhile; the *Chronicle* described the death struggles, and the making of a death-bed will in favor of the victim's lady love. The autopsy report followed, in which the reader was taken on a gory tour along the path of the fatal bullet and shown the damage done to the various internal organs.

But that was Wilcox's sole venture into sensational journalism. The next issue of the *Chronicle,* No. 14, dated June 2, 1895, was the last. In the announcement of its death Wilcox blamed lack of support as the cause of the journal's demise. This item appeared in the form of an obituary notice:

"DIED—In Jerome June 1st, 1895, *The Jerome Chronicle.* Interment in the newspaper graveyard. Please omit posies."

Herbert Eugene Wilcox came of a prominent family of New Bedford, Massachusetts. A cousin by marriage was Ella Wheeler Wilcox, famed poet and author. He went west to California where he made money by speculating in commodities. Other financial ventures dissipated his wealth; hoping to make a comeback in mining he went to Globe, where he worked for a period on the Silver Belt before deciding that Jerome was a greener pasture. After the failure of the *Chronicle* his friend George W. Hull made him secretary of his mining companies, a position he held until September, 1908. Ill health was the reason given for his moving to Los Angeles with his family.

Wilcox was three times married, first in the East, twice in Jerome. His first two wives divorced him on grounds of cruelty; the third, in California, sought a divorce but was denied the separation. She then left Wilcox, living alone with her daughter. One morning when he made a visit to her cottage and was denied admittance, he drew a pistol and shot himself. He left no property except a considerable assortment of mining stocks of little value.

The camp was not to be long without a newspaper. Later in 1895 William S. Adams began publication of *The Arizona Mining News,* and it and its successors continued publication for forty years.

A Canadian by birth, Adams became a printer in his teens, and on the road to Jerome worked at his trade in New York, Wisconsin, Colorado, and Prescott, Arizona. In Wisconsin and Colorado he had dabbled in politics, serving in county offices. He continued this interest in Arizona. In 1897 with H. J. Allen's blessing he was appointed chief clerk of the nineteenth territorial legislature, and was elected to the lower house of that body in 1899.

Adams knew how to get along. He allied himself with the Copper Company. He never crossed that corporation in any way, and was ever ready to praise it and its owners and management and to support its political favorites. In return he received financial support.

The name of the paper was soon changed to *The Jerome Mining News.*

Competition was not long in coming. In 1896 A. E. Jocelyn, a forty year old bachelor who taught school in Jerome, started publication of a weekly which he called *The Yavapai County Reporter.*

After he had started publication of the *News,* Adams added to his staff J. A. Thompson, a man with some newspaper experience. In 1897 Jocelyn took a wife and found the combination of marriage, teaching and newspapering too confining. He sold out to Thompson, who quit the *News* and sent for his brother, C. S. Thompson, to help him run the sheet. They changed its name to *The Jerome Reporter.*

In March, 1898, Adams converted the weekly *News* to a daily, but after two months he threw in the towel on that dream. His plant was destroyed by fire that fall, but he obtained new equipment and resumed publication.

It was also in 1898 that another weekly, *The Jerome Hustler,* entered the field under the proprietorship of D. D. McDonald, rumored to be a representative of a western newspaper chain.

Three newspapers were two too many for a little town. Predictably, animositities between the publishers took root and flourished. Name calling was rampant with no thought of suits for libel; there was more fear of personal encounter than of legal action. We are denied the full story of the editors' quarrels, as no copies of the *Hustler* are known to exist, and but few copies of the *Reporter.*

There has been found no account of physical clashes between the editors during this period, but there were a couple of instances where irate citizens, offended by news items, sought reprisal. At one time during a political campaign the Thompsons were forced to employ armed guards to prevent attacks by certain citizens who felt they had been libeled. In another instance, an assayer at the mine attacked McDonald with a hammer and left him with a bloody and aching head. We have many indications in *The Jerome Mining News* of Adams' animosity toward the Thompsons, some verbally violent; but we find nothing directly against the *Hustler* by Adams. He did, though, gladly publish a letter from a Jerome physician, Dr. Clark, to the *News* excoriating the editor of the *Hustler*, who had dared to infer that a diagnosis of skin disease made by the doctor in the case of a school boy was criminally wrong and alleging the diagnosis should have been for smallpox.

Dr. Clark wrote of McDonald that he was too lazy to work and too indolent to cultivate his maggot mind. He was not a newspaper man. He could not stick type, make up a form, or do press work. He was ignorant of the rudiments of education. His paper contained nothing but silly stories, meddlesome personalities, and verses such as none but a blubbering idiot could compose. Any schoolboy in knee pants was his master. He was *just no good,* said the doctor, who offered his apologies to the public for paying any attention to McDonald's Simple Simon paper or his cowardly self.

As to Bill Adams's opinion of the Thompson brothers, the following excerpts from an editorial give more than a hint:

> Jim Thompson is the youngest, the one who walks like the letter S, wears his hat on his nose and his mouth always open. Jim looks crooked, but it is his brother 'Clod' who engineers all their crooked work . . .

In another editorial Adams accused the Thompsons of being housebreakers and thieves, and of skullduggery in general. They were, Adams declared, fools, coyotes, crooks, reptiles, vultures, ignorant asses and bodily filthy.

But enemies or not, the *News* and the *Reporter* combined to absorb the *Hustler* in May 1900. McDonald got interested in mines, made money, and gave up newspapering.

The Thompsons abandoned Jerome in 1902, and Adams had the field to himself until 1907. In April of that year Frank E. Smith, in Jerome since 1903, purchased the *Reporter's* equipment and in partnership with his brother Ralph commenced publication of *The Jerome Copper Belt.* Ralph Smith was manager of the Jerome branch of the Bank of Arizona of Prescott.

The Smith brothers found no profit in this venture. In 1909 Frank was appointed postmaster of Jerome by President Taft, and the *Copper Belt* was sold to Mrs. I. P. (Laura) Nihell, wife of Jerome's principal plumber and tinsmith. After serving as postmaster for four years, until President Wilson appointed good Democrat William S. Adams to replace him, Frank set up a small job printing plant. He also served as justice of the peace.

The year 1909 was a comparatively quiet year for Jerome; there was only one murder that year. Looking about for an issue to discuss or a cause to promote, Bill Adams found it when Charley King, deputy marshal, wrote the paper a letter comdemning the Chinese restaurant operators for conducting filthy establishments. For the most part Adams had ignored the Chinese colony of Jerome, except to rail at its opium dens, but now he turned his dogs loose, and for quite a period of time spurred them to full cry. Specifically attacked was Charley Hong, who was accused of cleaning out the scrap boxes at the meat markets and using the refuse in his restaurant for making soups and stews even though it might be decomposed and fly-blown. Hong denied the charge, claiming that such scraps as he collected were used with other garbage for hog feed at his ranch in the valley.

Other Chinese restaurant operators were also accused of collecting refuse for their kitchens. The town council took notice. The health officer inspected. An order went out to all restaurants to clean up or close up. Two of them did close. But Adams was prepared to ride this black horse until it dropped; he collected and printed all remarks and items of information in derogation of the Chinese that he could obtain. Front page attacks were the rule. One man, it was reported, found maggots in his soup while eating at Hong's restaurant. Another report was that cockroaches and bedbugs had been found in the food. The Chinese, shouted Adams, should be barred from Jerome as they had been from other camps.

But the Chinese were not to be without their defender. The *Jerome Copper Belt* went to battle in their behalf. In her paper, the *News* reported, Mrs. Nihell printed a scathing attack against Charley King, accusing him of lying in his tirade against the Chinese for their alleged abuse of health standards. Space that had previously been given over to mining news was now used by Adams in attacks against Mrs. Nihell and her oriental friends.

Incensed at the *Copper Belt's* attacks against him, which the officer claimed involved even the members of his family, King entered suit against Mrs. Nihell for criminal libel.

The lady editor had at least one strong supporter, though; after the publication of one front page blast in the *News* her son sought out Adams and assaulted him. Adams's attacks subsided for four weeks, then a crude cartoon showing a woman supporting a Chinese was given front page space.

"Old Mother Petticoats," Adams titled it, "the woman with the serpent's tongue."

The Jerome Copper Belt continued publication until 1912, when Adams absorbed it, his paper after the deal appearing as *The Jerome News and Copper Belt.* Mrs. Nihell died in 1916.

A year after Adams received his appointment as postmaster he left the newspaper field. On his departure the Democratic party lost a strong booster, for Adams was rabidly partisan. He saw no good in the Republicans and in any of their acts or actions. The paper was loaded with debt, as the bank, on behalf of the United Verde, held a fistful of promissory notes covering the paper's physical assets. W. H. Archdeacon, auditor of the United Verde's two shortline railroads, took over the *News* early in 1914; Gaskell Romney was his manager. Three months later William F. Nicoll, an experienced newspaper man, took over with the backing of Ned Creighton, Phoenix politician, lobbyist, and publisher of a confidential news service. For three hundred dollars the paper and the debts went to them. The *"Copper Belt"* section of the name was dropped.

After his service as postmaster and justice of the peace Adams was given an easy watchman's job with the United Verde. For eighteen years he had served the company well. His health was beginning to fail, and he died in 1932 at age 74.

In July 1914 Nicoll sold his share of the publication back to Creighton, who placed J. M. Brackett in charge. In June 1916 Creighton sold out to Ernest Douglas and two associates, Charles DuBois and Millard E. Meloy. Dubois soon left, and in April 1917 Thomas D. Garlow became business manager. Phil Sinnott, from United Press, became editor, but soon he enlisted in the army, and to replace him Douglas brought in H. J. Minhinnick, who had been telegraph editor of *The Phoenix Gazette* and for a short period had been operating Dick Wick Hall's *Salome Bonanza Weekly.*

Minhinnick became editor, and Douglas took the title of manager.

The composing room and crew of The Jerome Mining News in 1914. William F. Nicoll, right, was proprietor.

Tom Garlow became advertising manager. Meloy left the paper in 1919.

With the entry of the United States into the world war in 1917 there was such a demand for war news that on May 1, 1917 publication of a daily was begun. The paper was renamed *The Verde Copper News.* It strongly supported the Republican party.

The new *News* was a good newspaper, competently edited. Douglas's pen was facile, both at prose and at verse. For some time he wrote a weekly section for his paper titled "Catclaws and Cactus Blossoms," which was received throughout the state as one of the most sparkling departments appearing in any of the Arizona newspapers. Minhinnick too was a versatile writer, and each issue of the *Copper News* contained wide double column editorials which covered the world. He could write on any subject, and did.

The new owners of the *News* had a clear field until 1916 when, on December 14, Lindley C. Branson published the first issue of *The Jerome Sun.* In April 1917 the paper became a tri-weekly; then, when it became known that the *News* would start a daily edition on May 1, Branson beat that paper to it by putting out the first issue of a daily on April 27, a four page seven column sheet.

During the early months of the *Sun's* life Branson felt his way, evidently attempting to establish his paper as a conservative and patriotic publication. He supported the government and the war, and avoided criticism of the United Verde Copper Company and his rival newspaper. But he needed additional financing, for neither circulation nor advertising, despite campaigns of solicitation, could match that of his rival by half. The *News* claimed a circulation of 6,000.

In the issue which proclaimed the *Sun's* expansion to a tri-weekly announcement was made that Edith Whitaker, a native Jerome girl whose father was pioneer Arthur Whitaker, had purchased a half interest in the *Sun* and would be its business manager. Her father and brother Fred associated themselves in the venture also. From that date there was a radical change in the paper's policy. It proved to be a fatal one.

An attack was begun upon the United Verde and all those coming under the big mine's influence, including business and professional men and some councilmen. Also coming under fire was *The Verde Copper News*, which the *Sun* chose to call *The United Verde Copper News*. During the 1917 strike, which slowed down mining in most of the Verde District mines, it accused the *News* of supporting the Industrial Workers of the World, the "Wobblies," or as some called them the "I Won't Workers"—a radical organization which had tried to insert itself into the negotiations between the miners' union and the mine operators.

James Douglas and his United Verde Extension Mining Company were spared criticism by the *Sun.*

During the year, attacks by Branson's paper against the United Verde and *The Verde Copper News* became more frequent. Among other things, it branded its rival paper "a corporation-owned newspaper prostitute."

The friends of Edith Whitaker, who were many, regretted to observe and were puzzled by the vindictiveness with which she attacked the United Verde, its officials and friends. She started a department in the Sun titled "United Verde Copper Company Column," in which she assailed the company and its general manager Robert E. Tally, the T. F. Miller Company—the "company store," some of the businessmen, and the members of the town council, who were accused of taking bribes. When in December, 1917, the council fired two of the town's police officers and the building inspector, replacing them with other men—including Fred Hawkins as deputy marshal—Branson and Whitaker started a move to have the councilmen recalled. It fell flat.

Tally was called "kaiser" in the Whitaker column, a deadly insult in those days of war, and also he was compared to a skunk with a yellow stripe down its back. One of the councilmen, W. P. Scott the undertaker, was accused of stealing gold fillings from the teeth of corpses.

Early in 1918, when it began to appear that the *Sun* was having financial troubles, villification of its human targets reached the front page. When at Clarkdale a United Verde deputized watchman shot and killed a man during some trouble, the *Sun* blared that this was a case of cold-blooded murder for which the Copper Company was responsible. One of the Branson-Whitaker team's favorite targets was Tom Garlow, advertising manager of the *News,* who was accused of being a "booze fighter" and of participating in an illegal gambling set-up in his paper's offices, and also of being a "hophead" and a peddler of dope and booze to the prostitutes on the line. Garlow filed a suit for both libel and slander against the *Sun's* owners for $15,000.

Up to this point the *News* had ignored the *Sun,* but now it announced that Ernest Douglas contemplated suing the *Sun's* owners, and that others who had been attacked, including state senator Charles H. Rutherford and deputy United States marshal Harry Carlson, planned similar action. Since Branson had begun publication of the *Sun,* the *News* said, he had followed a course such as might be expected of a professional blackmailer. He had claimed the *Sun* to be the organ of the labor unions, it was stated, but as he had been run out of Tonopah and Goldfield by the unions because he had slandered organized labor in the same way he had slandered businessmen in Jerome, such a claim made him out a liar.

The *Sun's* tirades extended even to Senator Clark; he and his United Verde were accused of being slackers in the war effort because copper production had not been largely increased. Actually, the smelter was operating at its full capacity.

That was too much for the Senator and his officials to take. With no warning, no *Sun* appeared on February 11, 1918. There was none on the 12th. On the 13th a five column edition appeared, which told a sad story. The *Sun's* newspaper press had been seized and carted away by agents of the thieving copper barons. But the *Sun* was not dead, Branson emoted. He had managed to obtain the loan of a small hand-power cylinder press from Clifford S. Klock, who down in Cottonwood published a small weekly called *The Cottonwood Leader.*

It developed that the promissory notes which covered the purchase of the *Sun's* press had been bought up by an agent of the United Verde, and some of them being overdue the press was removed under an action for sequestration. When Klock's press was brought to Jerome it was disclosed that he too owed money, and fearing that he also might have his press seized he hastily canceled his arrangement with the *Sun's* publishers and took his press back.

The *Sun* continued printing a small three-column sheet on a platen press for a couple of months, but on April 9, 1918, the last issue of the *Sun* was printed. Branson went away, and so did Edith Whitaker after awhile.

The Douglas-Minhinnick team ran *The Verde Copper News* until 1924, when Douglas decided to seek a broader field. He left Jerome and became associated with the *Mesa* (Arizona) *Journal-Tribune.* Subsequently he became managing editor of *The Arizona Farmer-Ranchman,* and at this writing he still steers that interesting journal. His writings on farm and irrigation problems and on conservation have been widely read and quoted. His column "Foxtail Johnson Objects" is syndicated. He has been honored and banqueted as the dean of Arizona newspapermen.

After Douglas's departure Minhinnick remained as editor of *The Verde Copper News*. Clarence R. Powell, bookkeeper, was promoted to business manager.

In 1926 A. J. Doud, a man experienced in the newspaper business, took over the *News* as publisher and in name the sole owner. Minhinnick remained as editor until March 1927, when he left the paper and was employed by the United Verde until ill health forced his retirement. He died in 1936. John C. McPhee was made editor. He was experienced and well qualified for the job, but he left in 1928. In the same year the United Verde acquired in Doud's name *The Prescott Journal-Miner*. Doud moved to Prescott but retained his nominal ownership of the *News*. The *Journal-Miner* subsequently was merged with *The Prescott Courier*.

After McPhee's departure A. V. Napier was appointed editor of the *News*. He lasted until July 1929, when he was replaced by Mostyn Lloyd, who died the following January. In February 1930 T. M. Pennington became managing editor and R. E. Smith news editor. In January 1931 Pennington left to become a partner in a Phoenix printing firm.

Carl E. C. Whitten, an energetic young man who for eight years, since his Jerome school days, had been an employee of the *News,* was made managing editor. In 1932 it reverted to a weekly. Whitten stayed with the paper until its last issue was printed in 1935. He then published *The Verde District Shopping News,* a give-away advertising sheet, for a time, then moved to Phoenix and built a printing business there.

Several attempts were made to establish a Spanish language newspaper in Jerome to serve the large Mexican population. In 1916 C. R. Dominguez started *El Clarin Disperso* in Jerome. It soon subsided. The next year he tried again under the name *Accion Logica. El Clarin Disperso* was revived in 1918, to suffer the same fate. Beginning in 1927 under the editorship of Francisco M. Sanora, and continuing for two or three years, the *Verde Copper News* published a weekly Spanish language insert.

In 1923 D. M. Lopez started a sheet he named *Don Quijote,* but it too died shortly after birth.

Other Verde Valley towns had to have their fling at newspapering. Clifford Klock's *Cottonwood Leader* didn't last long, but that didn't discourage R. C. Mitchell, who on October 9, 1920, published No. 1 of the *Cottonwood Clarion.* This too soon passed.

On November 5, 1930, the first issue of *The Camp Verde Enterprise* appeared, with George B. Young the editor. He became infused with the newspaper virus while acting as representative of *The Verde Copper News* for the lower valley. This paper was short lived.

Following the death of *The Verde Copper News* in 1935 the Jerome Chamber of Commerce published a weekly news bulletin, but this did not last long. This was the last attempt to give Jerome a news publication.

In 1930 Charles C. Robinson, a Jerome jeweler, was granted a license to operate a radio station, and in that year station KCRJ, a 100 "watter," went on the air. Having the depression to contend with the station had difficulties, and the equipment was eventually sold and moved from the valley.

So ends this account of early day communication media in Jerome and the Verde valley. Among those newspaper men who strove to put Jerome on the map were some sturdy characters and perhaps some queer ones. They all added to the color of a colorful community.

We owe a lot to the pioneer founders and editors of the frontier newspapers. They were as quick with their pens as the lawmen were with their guns. They kept their readers informed of as much of what was going on within and without those stirring communities as limited communication and prudence would allow. They were positive in their opinions and often ready to defend them with verbal bullets and bombs. They were ready to make the eagle scream, and just as ready to singe with vituperative fire the hair of an editorial opponent or business competitor.

But they did help to make and record history. Thanks are due them for that.

14

Murder, Mayhem and Marshals

Listening to the tales told by the old timers, one gained the impression that a lot of blood had been spilled in Jerome and its purlieus in the early days. They liked to tell of the shootin' deputies and marshals and of the reckless and usually unfortunate characters who ran afoul of them. They were not inclined to deny the claim, widely publicized around the turn of the century, that Jerome had been the wickedest city in America.

On the other hand, Jerome's boosters, especially its several newspapers, boasted that Jerome was really a peaceful town, with but little crime—even though in one year the town magistrate collected $14,000 in fines and imposed numerous jail sentences.

It being the purpose of this book to record the history of Jerome in as accurate a manner as possible, an effort has been made to reconcile the floating and divergent tales with the facts. In the process newspapers covering most of a forty year period, beginning with 1895, have been scanned. From this search we can account for about seventy-five homicides. Most surely there were a number of which we have no printed record, but which persistent recounting by long time residents has endowed with the aura of credibility. In the foreign quarter of the town there were countless battles with much mayhem and some resultant deaths, to which so little attention was given by the press that in some cases names were omitted.

The big killers of men in that period were the mines, few of which had adequate safety equipment or practices. Deaths in the mines exceeded the homicides probably by two to one.

The first Jerome murder to be reported in a local newspaper was the shooting of Charles Ward by Jake Brown in 1895, already mentioned in chapter 13. Accounts of a few other homicides which attracted more than usual attention will be given here. Additional ones have been told in the stories of the lawmen in GHOSTS OF CLEOPATRA HILL.

In 1900 there was a killing in the United Verde mine, interesting mainly for its aftermath. Rice D. Forman slew Franco Toniale by splitting his skull with a shovel, then took the cage to the surface and disappeared. During the following years Forman discovered he had a conscience, and the memory of his crime preyed upon his mind with increasing force. After sixteen years he could endure his guilt no longer; in California he surrendered to San Bernardino authorities and was returned to Arizona to take his punishment.

About two-thirds of the homicides in the Jerome area involved men who had immigrated from Mexico. In addition to the many Latin-Americans employed by the United Verde, when the United Verde Extension swung into production its owners imported from south of the border a considerable number of workmen who had gained experience in Mexican mines. A man who had spent many years in Mexico explained the larger role the Spanish-Americans played in the taking of life in this manner: First, the nature of those of the Latin-Indian amalgam is more volatile than of those of the northern races; second, the immigrants from Mexico had not the advantages of a broad education; and third, these people had been reared in a culture which fostered the belief that it was a man's privilege and duty to take care of his own problems without the interference of laws which might conflict with his birthrights. But the great majority of the Mexican people were of good character, and in Jerome there were a number of men among them with the qualities of leadership who had great influence in bringing to their countrymen a better understanding of the place they should take as responsible citizens of the community.

The so-called foreign quarter of Jerome, in which Mexicans predominated, was centered in the Deception Gulch area east of the business district, and extended north through Bitter Creek. Two of its main traffic ways were named for heroes of Mexico, Juarez and Diaz. The buildings were packed close together. This area was the scene of the story which follows:

"MAN, WOMAN DIE IN PUBLIC EXECUTION
AS HUSBAND KILLS BEFORE SYMPATHETIC MOB.
ETERNAL TRIANGLE CLIMAXED."

Those headlines capped the story of a double killing which appeared in the July 31, 1928, issue of *The Verde Copper News.*

"Led like stock to slaughter," the story began, "a man and a woman

Above: Marshal Johnny Hudgens standing on Main Street.
(Jerome Historical Society)
Below: Section of cemetery in East Jerome.

fell dead before the flash of a pistol as the unwritten law functioned in one of the most dramatic murders in the history of Jerome yesterday."

The principals in this affair were Victoriano Jiminez, 24, his wife Maria, 21, and Bernardo Ramirez, 23. The two men were miners. The Jiminez couple had two small children. The shooting occurred on Juarez Street.

It was common gossip in the quarter that Ramirez and Maria were having an affair. Jiminez was well liked; the sympathies of the people were with him, and he was told what was going on. Retribution appeared to be in order, and his friends encouraged him to proceed.

He got a gun and set up a watch. He caught his wife and Ramirez together. The woman fled to another house, but she was cornered by her husband's sympathizers and brought to the place where Ramirez was already held captive by Jiminez and his supporters.

A crowd had gathered and grown to mob proportions, and mob psychology began to prevail.

"Kill them!" came shouts from the crowd. "Show the world you are a man!" Some of the men had pistols; shots were fired in the air.

"Do it! Do it, Victoriano!"

Maria Jiminez tore herself loose from her captors and started to run. Jiminez shot her twice, killing her instantly. Then he turned on Ramirez and shot him twice in the head. Immediately afterward he disappeared.

Jerome police started an intense search for Jiminez, but it was fruitless. It was believed that friends had assisted in his disappearance, either keeping him in hiding or helping him to flee the area.

A departure from the usual manhunt in which the populace let the officers do it all, while at times even running interference, occurred in July, 1906, after Jesus Echeverria stabbed a man to death. We don't know the name of the victim, but the circumstances were such that public anger was aroused, and when marshal Fred Hawkins and deputy marshal Charlie King organized a manhunt and called for help there was a mass response. According to *The Jerome Mining News* "hundreds of men" joined in the most intensive search for a fugitive the valley had ever known. Those who could obtained horses, the others set out afoot, armed with rifles, shotguns and pistols. A report that the killer had been seen running toward the river sent horsemen that way in an effort to head him off, while the rest of the hunters spread out and flowed eastward over ridges and gulches.

Then came word that the fugitive had been turned back and was headed up Bitter Creek toward Jerome. That watercourse was promptly invaded. The killer was sighted, run down and surrounded; he dropped his knife and surrendered after viewing the encircling horde. Jerome's greatest manhunt was over.

As has been the case with several stories told me by early-day residents of Jerome, no mention of the following tale has been found in the Jerome newspapers, probably because of missing issues. Confirmation of a sort was given in the reminiscences of J. A. Thompson. The incident related occurred in the early 1900's, when Jim Roberts was marshal.

George Ward conducted a rooming house in Jerome. On several payday nights rooms of his tenants had been burglarized while he was absent or asleep. Having enough of this, on the next payday night Ward secreted himself in a room near the front of the house, armed with a shotgun. As if on schedule a man wearing a mask entered, slipped down the hallway and paused before Ward's own room. Ward cocked his gun; the man heard the click, and fled toward the entrance. As he ran past him Ward pulled the trigger and literally blew off the top of the burglar's head.

Unmasked, the man proved to be an Italian miner who unsuccessfully had been trying to date Ward's daughter. He was well known among the members of the sizeable Italian colony. A group of these men threatened retribution, claiming the dead man had only been trying to make a social call. They didn't bother to explain the mask.

A group of ten of the dead man's friends attended the funeral together in a rig having several seats. Jim Roberts knew them to be among those who had been making threats, and on their way back to town he stopped them.

"You fellows have been asking who gave Ward authority to take the law into his own hands and kill a man," he said. "Though it's none of your ___ _____ business I'll tell you. I gave him the gun, and told him to shoot anyone who tried to rob his place or molest him at any time. Don't let me hear of your making any more threats."

The rumblings died.

One of the most sensational murders in the town, and one of those remembered the longest, was the slaying of deputy marshal and constable Charley King on September 3, 1910. The murderer was N. B. Chavez, an ex-convict.

It was night. On patrol, King heard shots in the red light district north of the Hull Avenue business area. He at once went to the place where he believed the shots to have been fired. He was questioning a Mexican girl when from a house close by, the one in which Chavez lived, came two shots. One bullet struck the girl in the thigh, the other penetrated King's back.

The circumstances indicated that the officer had been deliberately ambushed. Chavez was immediately arrested by Fred Hawkins. King died four days after the shooting.

King was a popular man among the lawabiding element of the town, but hated by those who did not respect the law. Feeling in the town against Chavez ran so high that Hawkins, to avoid a lynching, hurried the killer to jail in Prescott. He was convicted of first degree murder and sentenced to hang.

In June 1912 Miguel Peralta shot and killed his ex-wife and her lover. He received the death sentence.

Though appealed to the supreme court the sentences of both Chavez and Peralta were upheld. Then George W. P. Hunt, new governor of the new state, who did not believe in capital punishment, issued reprieves to both men. Angry Jerome citizens held a mass meeting in protest. The state board of pardons and paroles did not go along with the governor and let the death sentences stand.

Jerome's next big murder sensation occurred on March 15, 1914. It was very nearly a double murder, and ended with the suicide of the man with the gun.

Guy H. Bailey was the young manager of the Jerome branch of The Bank of Arizona. He was associated with others in the subdivision and sale of tracts of land near Cottonwood. One of the purchasers of a tract was a Russian, Peter Naukijas, who had been employed in the United Verde smelter at Jerome. He declared to Bailey that he had been deeded a tract inferior to the one he had been promised. In an endeavor to adjust the matter Bailey, with Carl Heim, attorney for the subdividers, took Naukijas down to the tract in his car.

The Russian could not be satisfied. On the return to Jerome Bailey drove while Heim and Naukijas occupied the back seat of the car. As they reached the outskirts of Jerome the Russian pulled a pistol, shot Heim in the side of his face, then shot Bailey in the back of the head. He then sent a bullet into his own brain.

Rolling backward, the car turned into a bank and stopped. There the three were found. Bailey and Naukijas had died instantly. Heim was more fortunate; the bullet did not penetrate the brain but emerged through an eye.

Kosta Katich was a Serbian of a quarrelsome nature who operated one of the largest rooming houses in Jerome. In 1921 he and Emil Kovacovich, who operated a store, had an altercation over the amount of a bill Kovacovich had presented for supplies furnished. Upon Katich's refusal to pay, Kovacovich started suit, and he was at the town hall talking to officer Kirby when Katich entered, pistol in hand, and started shooting. Attempting to disarm Katich, Kirby was shot in both thighs, and Kovacovich was shot in a shoulder and a leg. Katich served a jail sentence.

Katich was good at making enemies, and four years later he paid the price. One night in 1925 while Katich was in his office talking to another person a masked man entered and ordered the two to throw up their hands. Katich's visitor complied with all possible speed. Katich did not, whereupon he was shot fatally.

The murderer disappeared, and no clue was found as to his identity.

Down in the Verde Valley there was some bloodletting of great interest to the people of Jerome. In Camp Verde, on a midsummer night in 1899, a man walked out of the dusk and shot to death Clint Wingfield and Mack Rodgers at the general merchandise store which they operated in partnership. Jerome's interest was due in part to the fact that the man who took the killer's trail was sheriff John Munds, who had been a deputy sheriff in Jerome and who was the son of that town's mayor William Munds. The sheriff trailed the supposed killer on horseback and afoot for 1400 miles, winding up in New Mexico where he found the man he was after to be already in custody after an abortive single-handed effort to rob a train.

Another murder which attracted wide attention was perpetrated at the ranch near Jerome owned by A. S. Haskell and John Kirwagen. They were orchardists and gardeners, their irrigation water supplied from a copious spring. Kirwagen had an altercation with Al Cowles, a ranch hand. Cowles made threats, and later entered the ranch house, found Kirwagen, and shot him. He next found Haskell at the barn, confessed to the murder, and then killed himself. Kirwagen's daughter Rose subsequently married William Holliday, Jerome businessman, and for many years was chief operator of the Jerome telephone exchange.

The spring, known to this day as the Haskell spring, since 1912 has been the source of the fine mountain water Clarkdale enjoys.

In November 1906 Jerome and the valley were excited by an affair which left six men dead. Justin Head, a Camp Verde Apache, was an educated Indian who, because of his command of the English language, was at times called to Prescott to act as interpreter at superior court trials. After one such appearance an Indian who had been tried and convicted for robbery, after his jail term had been served met Head in Cottonwood and accused him of falsely interpreting his testimony. A fight ensued in which Head killed his accuser. According to testimony given by Head later, after the fight he left for Camp Verde to surrender to the authorities there, but word of the killing preceded him and upon his arrival in Camp Verde he was met by a band of Indians bent on avenging the death of Head's victim. They attacked Head who, armed with a rifle, killed four of his opponents, and shot his own brother, accidentally, he claimed, in the arm. From this injury the brother died.

Head went into hiding, but the story was circulated that he was going on a rampage, planning to kill as many men as he could before he himself was killed. This caused many Indians to flee to Jerome for protection by the officers there.

A large posse was organized by the sheriff to hunt Head down, but they found no trace of him, though the hunters included several former Indian scouts and white men skilled in tracking. The slippery fugitive might never have been caught had he not decided to give himself up. Several days later he slipped into Jerome and surrendered to marshal Fred Hawkins, who rushed him to jail in Prescott.

Preceding the so-called insurrection of Mexican renegades in 1918, James Lowry, famed Arizona peace officer, was shot and killed by Porfirio Hernandez. Lowry was in the employ of the United Verde Extension smelter as a deputized guard. He had served three terms as sheriff of Yavapai County and was widely known. The Extension company offered $2500 for the person of Hernandez, dead or alive. The reward was claimed a few days later by Frank Dickinson, Camp

Verde rancher, who encountered the fugitive near his ranch and killed him.

To add a touch of the old West to the more modern scene, in 1923 Harry Garrison Hall and Robert L. Johnson had a real old fashioned, rip-roarin' shoot-out down in Cottonwood. Johnson was killed and Hall seriously injured.

There were affairs regarding which family and friends preferred silence. On a hunting trip near Jerome with two brothers and a third man in the party, the brothers, members of a prominent family, had a violent quarrel over a lost gun. A shooting followed, in which one of the brothers shot the other in the arm, inflicting a wound from which he subsequently died. Then the third man shot and killed the unwounded brother. In another family quarrel a man shot and killed his brother-in-law.

Knifings and other injuries inflicted in physical combat but not resulting in death were frequent in Jerome, but seldom mentioned by the press except when unusual circumstances or serious injury were involved. Such as the scrap during which Ben Moore bit off his opponent's ear. Ben was charged with mayhem, found guilty, and sentenced to three years and six months in the hoosegow.

Of course, if it was only a man's wife against whom an act of violence was committed, the husband didn't need to fear incarceration. One named Petchauer who lived down in the gulch beat his wife nearly to death. After she was taken to the hospital Petchauer was arrested, charged with simple assault and fined ten dollars.

Then there was the case of L. W. Watson, a "Jack the Ripper" type of character, who decided to punish Fannie Howard, inmate of a bawdy house, claiming that the service she sold was of low quality. When she refused to return his money he slashed her face and neck so severely it took ninety-one stitches to put her together again. We have found no account of what the law did to Watson.

Jerome had all the underlying tensions which could have made it a really bloody town. But it also had some marshals and deputies who were not afraid to kill or beat into submission the unruly and the belligerent, and knowledge of this most certainly prevented many more crimes from being committed than actually occurred.

It is not with pride that we relate the stories told in this chapter. They are recorded that those of later generations may know what life in and near Cleopatra Hill was like in "the roaring days." To look back is the only way the history of Jerome may be understood, for as a mining camp it sleeps now.

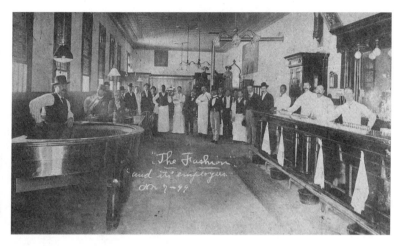

Above: The interior of the Fashion Saloon. (Jerome Historical Society)
Below: The Club in the Boyd Hotel. (Jerome Historical Society)

15

Bars, Chips and Moonshine

The historian who wrote that the big fire of 1898 burned down twenty-four saloons and fourteen Chinese restaurants probably exaggerated. Of saloons there were many, but it is doubtful if Jerome ever harbored more than fifteen at one time. Soon after the town was incorporated in 1898 the city fathers ordained that no more than twelve liquor licenses should be issued, and from then on saloons which could legally operate within the incorporated area were limited to that number. In 1911 the number was reduced to eight. Outside the municipal boundaries there were places where liquor could be bought and where gambling and women could be found.

Only once in the earlier years of the municipality was there a town election without one or more saloon keepers among the successful candidates. On the first council, appointed by the county supervisors in 1898 was Arthur Cordiner; the second in 1900, Charley Hooker; in 1902, Dave Connor; in 1904, Fred Ullman; in 1908, both Hooker and Connor; in 1910, Connor; in 1912 and 1914, Cordiner. But by 1916 the anti-saloon, anti-gambling, and anti-women element had become strong enough to stop the election of any saloon keepers to the council.

The so-called "wide open" saloons of Jerome's early years were in fact wide open. Gambling flourished. Girls were regularly employed by several of the houses, particularly by the Fashion, which had a stage on its main floor and imported troupes of entertainers. The Fashion was "big business" according to the standards of the times. When it first opened in its new building in 1899 it had two crowded floors, the basement being used as a "family" spot, with private booths where a man and a woman could lunch and drink alone. There were games here too, and a bar.

In 1903 the Fashion's business had grown so large that additional space was needed. Hoover and Cordiner rented the Senate saloon next door, the building later known as the Kentucky Tavern. They cut a door through the concrete wall between the two establishments. Installed in this large new space were eleven gambling games, including faro, craps, roulette, monte, stud poker, and a Chinese lottery. Though this became the main gambling room, games were still carried on in the original building.

In its write-up on the expansion *The Jerome Mining News,* with typical hyperbole, boasted that "the New Fashion Saloon and Gambling House is the largest and most complete establishment of its kind in the Southwest, if not on the continent." The Fashion employed fifty men and women, the *News* reported.

At that time nine saloons were advertising their goods and services in the *News.* Influenced by the widely circulated and locally deplored stories of Jerome's wickedness, and the growing awareness of many of its citizens that the town would benefit by a moral cleansing, in 1905 the town council ordained that effective January 1, 1906, gambling would be barred. The gaming houses joined to fight the ordinance, declaring it to be defective and illegal. The county attorney agreed and ruled that the ordinance could not be enforced, and the county sheriff began issuing licenses to the saloons when the town council refused to do so.

The town then had another ordinance drafted in which an attempt was made to correct the faults alleged in the first. Still the gamblers refused to close their games. The three largest operators, Arthur Cordiner, Phil Pecharich and Charles Hooker, planned an action which would bring the matter to a court test. They rented a vacant basement, placed a table and chairs, and while suspending gambling in their regular places of business started a stud poker game in the new location. By this maneuver they avoided the danger of having their regular gaming equipment confiscated.

Cordiner, Pecharich and Hooker were promptly arrested by Fred Hawkins, and brought to trial before a jury of twelve in Jerome's justice of the peace's court. The defendants employed Reese M. Ling, a lawyer prominent in Prescott and later in Phoenix. (His son Perry became Jerome's city attorney twenty years later.) Ling's defense was based on a technicality: councilman M. J. Foley had resigned from the council prior to the passage of the last anti-gambling ordinance, and S. S. Cunningham had been chosen by the council to replace him. Ling contended that the council had no such authority, and that therefore the body of the council was illegally constituted. The territorial legislature had passed a law giving a town council authority to elect a replacement in case of a vacancy, but Ling proved that law had not yet become effective when Cunningham was elected. The jury acquitted the gamblers.

When a new council took office in May 1906 it promptly passed another anti-gambling ordinance. J. S. Hoover of the Fashion announced that he would not comply with it and he kept his games open. Arrested and convicted, he carried his case to the Arizona supreme court, whose decision, written by Chief Justice Richard E. Sloan, was that the Jerome ordinance was invalid.

Included in the ordinances which had been declared invalid was a provision barring women from saloons. Fred Hawkins did remove them temporarily.

But legal gambling in Arizona was doomed. In 1907 the territorial legislature passed a law prohibiting gambling. By the same act women were barred from saloons.

The business of saloon keeping without gambling looked bad to Hoover and Cordiner. They sold the Fashion to John Keller and Company, but later Cordiner came back from California and reclaimed the business.

As in other places, everywhere, national, state, or local laws didn't stop gambling or other illicit occupations. Fred Hawkins and his brother officers did temporarily place checks on violators. They raided games in saloons and other places, but gambling went on.

In the state election of 1914 saloons were voted out. Gambling was then transferred mainly to pool halls. In 1918 Hawkins raided a game in the basement of the Arizona pool hall that netted a haul of eight. Fines of $100 were levied; if the gamblers could not pay, they went to jail. The council ordered all card games of any kind closed. All slot machines were ordered removed.

In 1919 two pool halls were raided, the Palace and Paz and Cota. Four arrests were made in each place, all drawing $100 fines. The Palace was later raided again, also the Fischer pool hall; sixteen were arrested. The proprietors drew $150 fines, the players $100 each.

In 1922 the council ordered a clean-up campaign on the grounds that Jerome had become known as such a good place for gamblers that it was attracting professionals. Eight tinhorns were floated out of town, two others jailed.

The council ordered strict enforcement of the decree that all card games must be closed. But gambling in Jerome was never stopped. One could always find a card game and plenty to drink during the period this story covers.

When the saloons were closed by state law a new industry was born in the Verde Valley, as elsewhere. The valley became one of the most prolific bootleg liquor producing areas in the state. The sheriff assigned deputies to Jerome, and a deputy United States marshal was stationed there, but as stills were found and demolished others took their place. The natural facilities for concealment were many, including old mine tunnels and other remote and hard to reach spots. Ingenuity was used in finding concealed places in which the distillers might conduct their enterprises. Sections of basements were walled off, with no visible access. In a recent year when the purchaser of a vintage house in Jerome undertook a remodeling job, he opened up a small room which had had no access except through the attic, and which housed a small still and other equipment.

Knowing that white mule was being produced somewhere in the neighborhood of Peck's Lake, Fred Hawkins made searches over a period of time. He looked in caves and even waded the marshes of the lake where the tules grew tall. Though the location seems improbable, he finally decided to explore the tunnel which brought water from the Verde River to the ranches around the lake; an enterprise of Dan Shea early in the century. The tunnel was 1000 feet long and carried a flow of water four feet deep. The outlet of the tunnel surfaced in a little gulch. With hip boots and a lantern Fred went wading. He found where a cavern had been excavated above the tunnel timbering, and in the cavern was a still and the ingredients necessary in the manufacture of liquor.

In the 1920's the liquor industry flourished, both in manufacturing and marketing. Spurred on by the United States Marshal and his deputies, county and local officers of the law sped up their efforts to apprehend the bootleggers and close the speakeasies. According to the press, in September 1923 there were fourteen arrests in the Jerome area and eighteen in October. Still the flow of booze increased. Loud outcries were made upon the discovery of some stills operated under conditions almost unbelievably filthy. But trying to scare the imbibers didn't have much effect, although there was sickness, even death, from drinking some of the stuff.

Late in 1926 a still was found in East Jerome that was "one of the finest and most complete that we have ever encountered," according to Jack Crowley, Jerome's chief of police.

The officers gave the appearance of doing the best they could, but there was a mighty large and rough country to cover. Liquor still flowed in, some of it pretty good stuff, according to imbibers; a gallon of real tasty 100 proof moonshine could be bought for twenty-five dollars, if one knew where to go—and everyone knew. Stills continued to be built bigger and better. In 1928 local officers assisted in the capture at Cherry Creek, south of Jerome, of what was claimed to be the largest still ever discovered in Arizona—its capacity was 450 gallons. Then over on Oak Creek two fine large stills were captured about the same time.

One of the big events of the social season in Jerome was the annual ball of the volunteer fire department. Each such event was a real jamboree. The story has been told over and over again that to provide the required liquid refreshments an officer who was a member of the fire department would raid enough blind tigers to provide the needed amount to make the largely attended event really successful. One longtime resident nostalgically asserted that twenty gallons was the usual take.

The officers were too busy to pay much attention to the hundreds of citizens who brewed their own beer and fermented their own wine. Yeast and malt syrup were two of the best selling commodities at the stores. Raisins and sugar too.

A residue of prohibition days was a host of stories growing out of that noble experiment. Some no doubt had their origins in actual happenings, others were obviously apocryphal. We give here two stories, placing one in each class.

A man out of work in the 1920-1921 shutdown made himself a still by using a large teakettle and adding attachments. A lot of Jerome-ites were taking similar action, either to supply their own needs or to bring in a few dollars, but this man was reported by a neighbor as a lawbreaker and he was arrested.

When brought before the magistrate he burst into tears, and sobbed out a most pitiful tale. His wife, he said, was sick; he had three little children who went hungry except when, by whatever means possible, he was able to bring in enough money to buy food. The children needed clothes; he was without firewood.

The judge was so moved by this heartrending tale that he cried a little too, and dismissed the prisoner with a reprimand. Whereupon he went happily back to his teakettle.

The other story concerns a hardy soul who stashed a still high up a steep ridge in an abandoned mine tunnel, to which he hauled up his grain and other materials on his back. He used gasoline for fuel. Once when he had gone to town his burner sprang a leak and his plant blew up. When the operator returned he found the blast had exposed a vein of good ore.

With that unlikely tale we'll close this chapter and travel on.

Mine Museum of Jerome Historical Society—Former Fashion Saloon. Photo by Herb Young.

16

The Madams and the Girls

The question has been asked "What would a mining camp have been like without its feminine entertainers and its demimonde?"

Any speculation regarding such a situation most surely would have no empirical basis, for every camp busy enough to support a store, a restaurant, and a saloon, would inevitably have its women.

Jerome's women came early and stayed long. A resident who had lived in Jerome through its most active days told this writer that in its heyday there were as many as one hundred and twenty women in the camp's redlight district and its scattered bordellos. That may have been an overestimate, but Jerome had a lot of "the girls."

In the earlier days of the camp there were houses in the center of the business district where women of easy virtue dwelt. Prior to the big fires Japanese Charlie operated a place on Jerome Avenue, only three doors removed from the Connor Hotel; ostensibly his place was a restaurant and a rooming house. North of the Connor on Main Street there were so many lodgings for the girls that the area was known as "the tenderloin district." The principal madam in that section was Jennie Banters, who owned her own two-story building and was claimed by some—though probably without supporting statistics—to be the richest woman in northern Arizona.

The women weren't often mentioned in the newspapers, but Bill Adams in his *Jerome Mining News* seemed to take a wry pleasure mentioning Jennie now and then, apparently the only one of her profession given that distinction. "Jennie is back in town." "Jennie is the first one on north Main Street to start rebuilding after the fire." Et cetera.

Jennie was burned out in each of Jerome's three big fires. While others were struggling to raise money to rebuild after the 1897 and 1898 fires Jennie quickly replaced her buildings, the replacements being as flimsily built as the original frame structure. But after the 1899

106

conflagration she rebuilt more substantially. In that fire, it was reported, she lost furs and jewelry worth three times the value of the building.

She was to have another fire to plague her, which started in the room of one of the girls. It was put out just in time to save the business district from another catastrophe. Again she came into notice when one of her girls was knifed to death, after which her assailant committed suicide. Jennie was the first property owner in the business district to build a sidewalk in front of her building. Through such actions the town could not forget that Jennie was there.

Though we have found no mention of them in the newspapers of the period, the names of four other madams have been given this scribe by old timers who recalled the gossip of the early days. There were Rose, a lady of dark complexion and fine appearance; Lily, whose name alone seems to have lingered in memory; Madam Pearl, remembered with gratitude by many men whom she helped when they were in need; and the Cuban Queen, tall, dark and handsome. As to their personalities, little is known other than that Madam Pearl was generous, and that she was an inveterate smoker, never without a cigaret even when she was at work. Her popularity extended even beyond the circle of her patrons. When she died in Jerome, prematurely, her body lay in state at the funeral parlor for twenty-four hours. That's what the old timers said, anyway.

Then it was said that the Cuban Queen chose her girls to match her own fine appearance. Several of them found husbands in Jerome. She did too. When the redlight district was finally closed she married a mine foreman. Invariably when a man took a wife from the line the couple moved away where the woman's regeneration could be accomplished among strangers.

"They made good wives," one man said who had allegedly been in touch with some of those who had found mates . . . "They had to try so much harder than those who had no brands to blot."

The Jerome town council was never free of the problem of the women. The church groups did not let the members forget. Under the mayorship of George W. Hull in 1905 women were barred from saloons. Later in that year the prostitutes were ordered to close up their retreats and get out of town. Fred Hawkins, before year's end, reported to the council that the cleanup had been completed, a report which appears to have been somewhat optimistic.

Above: Remains of "the cribs" on Hull Avenue,
circa 1970.
Below: Jennie Banters and her girls on the balcony of Jennie's Place, circa
1898. (Jerome Historical Society, Misenheimer Col.)

THE MADAMS AND THE GIRLS

After the new council elected in 1906 passed an ordinance prohibiting gambling in Jerome, the fact that it was ruled invalid was an encouragement to those ready to defy the council. Many of the women who had gone away returned and resumed business. The council then announced they would permit the women to stay on the condition that they register and report for physical examination twice monthly. A redlight district was established by the council within the boundaries of which the women must remain. This district was on north Hull Avenue to the rear of the upper Main Street business houses. A line of brick apartments, well constructed by Jerome standards of the time, were built, some of three story height. Across the street several frame structures were put to the same use. According to the newspaper there were forty women there, but the old timers laughed at that.

The Wigwam saloon had a place on the line, too.

In 1917 all redlight districts were closed as a war measure, and the girls were ordered out of town. Some left. Others stayed and engaged in private enterprise. There were so many scattered through the Deception Gulch area that it came to be known by a lewd name, accompanied by the criticism that had the girls been allowed to remain in their establishments, with health supervision by the town physician, it would have been much better for Jerome.

The restrictions were lifted at war's end and the line became active again. But opposition to a district practically in the center of town was strong.

For the most part in the years between the wars Jerome's newspapers seldom made any mention of the girls, but once in awhile they made news, as in an instance when the meaning of "tooth and nail" was illustrated. Two girls of the line had a knock-down, drag-out battle in which one of them was so badly bitten that she was disfigured. Two other girls, Myrtle and Trixie, the paper designated them, had a terrific battle over two men. (That's what it said. Perhaps one man apiece was not enough.)

A story was told this writer by the late A. B. Peach about a fight he witnessed between two hostesses at the Fashion somewhere around 1900. A young man of the town took a chance on a raffle in which a fine gold watch was the prize. While in a high condition he promised each of two girls, on different occasions, that should he win the watch it would be hers. He did win it, whereupon both girls claimed it.

A fierce battle resulted. A ring was formed about the screaming, writhing girls. In the fracas they lost their pretty dresses and most of their other apparel. When both were nearing exhaustion the onlookers stopped the fight, declaring it to be a draw. The girls had nothing more to fight about, anyhow, as the young man had hastily departed during the scrap, taking the watch with him, and he didn't come back.

The following story has a plot which may be familiar to many, and is related here only because it is true. It is told by a man, still living, who in his younger years worked for a Jerome drug store and made deliveries throughout the town, including the redlight district.

One of the women of the district had a daughter who had been placed in a private school in the East. Her mother had told her that she worked in a hotel in Jerome; the girl had no inkling of her parent's real profession. The daughter saved enough money from her allowance to make the trip to Jerome, and wrote the mother that she was coming. The woman was panic stricken and sought advice of friends who managed to find a job for her in one of the town's hotels. The daughter came, visited and went away without ever suspecting that her mother had another occupation.

Jerome's redlight district was a victim of the trend of the times—the activities of the churches and other religious and civic groups, individual citizens, and the men who made the laws. The feeling grew that such an openly conducted and centrally located industry demeaned the reputation of a town which was trying to claim a place among clean and progressive communities. As an example of protests based on moral grounds, when a school teacher discovered that members of her adult night language class were visiting the district after their evening studies, she was outraged and presented to the council a petition, signed by nearly all of the town's teachers, demanding that these dens of iniquity be closed.

An accompanying illustration shows the appearance of the remaining "cribs" in the present day. Many visitors wander down to see them—it is only a two minute walk from the mine museum on Main Street. Across the narrow street trees are growing tall and shading the spots where stood other houses, now gone. The interiors of the standing buildings have been wrecked; doors and windows stand open to the elements.

Those who are curious enough to venture inside find nothing to remind them of the perfumed bowers which once were the refuges of lonely men; but to the imaginative the soft sound of the little breezes which curl around the battered cornices may suggest the whisperings of ghosts—the spirits of those ladies who once hung out the welcome sign, then vanished into darkness.

Two prostitutes next to the Hull Avenue Cribs, circa 1920.
(Jerome Historical Society, Vickers Col.)

17

Fun, Games and Stuff

Jerome in its early days, isolated from the rest of the world by mountains on every side, had to make its own fun or ship it in. As entrepreneurs in entertainment enterprises she did pretty well.

Aside from the amusements to be found in the saloons and more private places, there were the sports peculiar to a mining camp as well as the more common ones.

As an example, the miners had their drilling teams. A huge granite boulder may be seen on Jerome's Main Street, filled with drill holes, reminder that on Independence Days or Labor Days individuals and teams from the mines strove to determine who, with single and double jacks, could drill the farther in the hard rock in a given number of minutes. In the team drilling one man would hold the bar of drill steel while the other wielded a sledge hammer, or two hammer wielders would take alternate blows at the head of the drill. This all took high skill. There was seldom a slip, though occasionally there would be accidents. Fingers would be mashed; in one instance at least the skull of a teammate was crushed. The single jackers had it safer, and had at it with a drill in one hand and a hammer in the other.

There were also mucking contests, where one man or a team vied with others to see who could shovel a given amount of crushed rock into a box in the shortest time.

An example of what activities the people of Jerome engaged in when they planned holiday amusements may be found in the program of the "grand celebration" staged on the Fourth of July, 1900.

A special event was the hose races between Jerome's two teams and teams from other towns. Next were the rock drilling contests. There were foot races for young and old, sack races, potato races, burro races, and various other contests especially for the young and young of heart, including the always popular scramble for the greased pig.

Several teams, each made up of men of different nationalities, competed in tugs of war. Even the Apache Indians brought in teams for

112

the contest. In the general revelry the possibility of race riots was ignored. At night the Apaches staged a war dance by firelight.

The celebration committee was not daunted by Jerome's hillside position when it staged a bronco riding contest. They found a corral below a livery stable well padded with stable cleanings to form a cushion for those who took to the air.

There was also a trap shooting contest.

In tribute to flag and country there was a patriotic meeting at the opera house, at which Henry D. Ross was orator. In later years he was to become chief justice of the state supreme court.

An annual event of note was staged by the Mexican population—the Cinco de Mayo fiesta, an annual celebration which was to become one of the principal public events of the town.

And of course there was a lot to eat and drink.

Jerome was particularly proud of its hose teams, and they started practicing to develop winning teams as soon as the fire lines were laid. The object of a hose race was to see which of the teams in contest, each drawing a two wheeled cart with a reel of hose, could make the fastest time in racing to a hydrant, coupling the hose and getting water through it. Tom Campbell was captain of a prize winning team. In 1907 Jerome sent a team to contest in Prescott's big Fourth of July celebration; this team won against teams from all over northern Arizona. In the flush of victory they issued a challenge to the world to compete against them. So loud was the challenge that it even was announced in a New York newspaper.

There were three bowling alleys at different periods in Jerome. The first, in the basement of the Kentucky saloon, was operated by Fred Whitaker. An effort was made to form a ladies team, but the thought of females indulging in such a sport, especially in the basement of a saloon, was so shocking that the attempt fell flat on its face.

Horseshoe pitching was a common sport, and many team contests developed.

Two athletic clubs had brief lives. A damper was placed on the activities of one club when a contestant in one of its boxing matches died from injuries received during the fight.

Baseball seemed an unlikely sport in the mountainous country in which Jerome is located, but the playing of America's national game

Above: A Jerome Volunteer Fire Department team training for a championship match in 1900. The lanky young captain in the lead is Tom Campbell, to become Arizona's second state governor.
Below: Dynky Lynx miniature golf course, circa 1930, in what is today Jerome's upper park. (Jerome Historical Society, Vladich Col.)

would not be denied the younger men. Jerome had its ball teams while the town was still a-building after the big fires.

Down on Will Jordan's ranch, below the site where the Clarkdale smelter was built years later, was a flat piece of unirrigated land on the west bank of the Verde. It's still there, just north of Clarkdale's patio town, nestled against the huge slag dump. The boys of the opposing teams would pile into wagons and drive down to this spot, mark out a diamond, and go to it. The teams were made up of miners, smeltermen, mechanics, merchants, office men—there was no difficulty in finding young men anxious to engage in physical sports, of which they had so few. They devised a method of stimulating the competitive spirit: a keg of beer was set up back of home plate; a team could drink only if at the end of an inning it had scored. If the team at bat was scoreless, the opposing team would be rewarded. But there was seldom an inning without scoring, and as the game progressed runs became increasingly more frequent. Some astonishing scores were made.

After the Clarkdale smelter commenced operation in 1915 a keen rivalry developed between Clarkdale and Jerome. The United Verde Copper Company fostered this as a segment of their plan to make life interesting for the employees and keep them from migrating. During the prosperous days of the twenties thousands of dollars were spent on facilities for outdoor sports. The Southwest was combed for skilled ball players who were given sinecures and other benefits. Arizona had a strong baseball league then, and among the state teams Jerome and Clarkdale were at the top and vying for the state championship. Jerome won it one year, Clarkdale another.

The company created a ball field with a grandstand at the western edge of Clarkdale. Jerome demanded equal treatment. The company always strove for balance between the communities, so a ball park Jerome would have. Up above the mine levels the top of a ridge was bulldozed off, and with waste material from the steam shovel operation a gulch was filled. A grandstand was built. Clark Field came into being. Now Jerome didn't have to depend upon the facilities of its hated rival for its practice sessions and interclub games.

Some genuinely high class talent was obtained for both the Jerome and Clarkdale teams, so good that in several instances players went on to the big leagues.

Above: The first Jerome baseball team to claim the championship of Northern Arizona.
Below: Swimming pool on the 300 level, circa 1928.
(Jerome Historical Society, L. Franquero Col.)

Friction began to develop between the teams. The Jerome team left a game unfinished because of a dispute over an umpire's call. Clarkdale's manager stopped a game because it was claimed that players from other state teams had been used on Jerome's team under assumed names. Cool heads among the game's supporters got the teams playing again.

Then Jerome hatched a coup which made Clarkdale again yell "foul!" They got Hal Chase on their team, and made him captain.

Hal Chase, as all old time ball fans well remember, had been a famed star of a Chicago big league team before he had been fired in a scandal which shook the baseball world, and he had been barred from ever again playing in organized baseball. So he was available for any minor team which could offer sufficient inducements. Jerome supplied those inducements; the public never knew the details of the arrangement.

Whatever Hal Chase was or had been he could play and coach baseball as few men could. He whipped the Jerome team into an almost unbeatable group. This intensified the growing ill feeling between the two towns; loud were Clarkdale's accusations that the only way Jerome could win was by employing crooks. At the games there were brawls among the spectators. Even the ladies got into the scene with hat snatching, hair pulling and name calling. Betting was heavy—so heavy that the *Verde Copper News* featured an editorial condemning it.

The United Verde officials looked with aversion at the monster they had helped to create, as the result of their support was just the opposite of what they had planned. The company withdrew its contributions to the individual teams and ordered them consolidated into one Verde Valley team. Players who didn't care for honest-to-goodness working jobs were dismissed.

Hal Chase was not among the players who stayed on. He was fired from his hospital job after he had been accused of pilfering supplies.

The high schools of the two towns also had keen rivalry, and each developed fine football, basketball and track teams. Each school had a well stocked trophy room.

The depression and the 1931 shutdown of mining and smelting operations ended all but moral support by the company of a ball team. Jerome and Clarkdale combined to field a team of sorts for several years, its only help being what it could solicit from the local citizens.

When softball came into popularity each of the valley towns had its teams.

One of the earliest of Jerome's major sports was trapshooting. With quail in abundance in the valley, and nearly everyone having gained some skill at wing shooting, there developed a group of expert clay pigeon busters. The best of the shooters formed a team which soon gained the championship of northern Arizona, whereupon they characteristically issued a challenge to the whole Southwest. No great glory resulted.

In 1916, stimulated by Pershing's incursion into Mexico and the growing menace of Germany's submarine warfare, a group of Jerome and Clarkdale men organized a rifle club. Others joined in flocks. One hundred and twenty-five men ordered Springfield and Krag rifles through the National Rifle Association, and requisitioned 30,000 rounds of free ammunition. When the War Department received this request the brass was alarmed; it must mean, they thought, that a company of irregulars was preparing to invade Mexico, where Villa was raiding. The order was held up. Carl Hayden, then Arizona's representative in the House, was appealed to, and being an expert rifle shooter and having captained Arizona rifle teams in the national shoots at Camp Perry, he intervened and the guns and ammunition came through.

A rifle range with standard carriers and targets was built on what was believed to be Copper Company land near Clarkdale, and the sport got under way, attracting wide attention and new members. The range couldn't accommodate all the shooters, so the Jerome members formed their own club, and the United Verde built them a range down the hill from the camp. It was constructed with the aid of dynamite over ridges and gullies; as was the case with the Jerome ball field, enthusiasm and money laughed at difficulties.

The Clarkdale club ran into trouble when it was found that the range had not been built on company land, but on the claim of a homesteader. After a nice clubhouse had been erected, he came around, thanked the boys for building him such a nice house on his land, but said that as he was subdividing the range must be vacated. The community of Centerville south of Clarkdale occupies the old range site now.

The homesteader permitted the club to sell the house to Fred Hawkins, employed by the United Verde Extension after he had been fired by the United Verde. When the war was over a new range was built two miles up the river, but it was hard to reach and the club and its facilities fell into a state of desuetude.

Prior to the birth of Clarkdale little thought had been given to the possibility of playing the "royal and ancient" game of golf in this mountainous land; then, with the United Verde offering the use of land on which a course of sorts could be built, interest began to grow. A golf club was organized. As with any innovative move that must crash frontiers, the members had to contend with the psychological opposition of a number of self-proclaimed rugged individuals who engaged only in manly sports, from which category they excluded golf. They professed to feel only sorrow for the sissies who wasted time and energy in chasing a little ball across country. But the members of the club were among the most prominent residents of the district—company officials, business and professional men, and other white collar workers composed the majority of the group, though membership was open to all.

The land which the company set aside for the golf course, across the Verde River from Clarkdale, was typical desert country, covered with mesquite, catclaw, greasewood, cactus and rabbit bush. Also with rocks. But the club members accepted the challenge presented. Two young men from England—Geoff and Bert Williams, brothers, who had had experience with golfing in the old country, aided in laying out the course and later each was to act as the club pro. On Sundays the members would descend on the course with axes, picks, shovels, rakes and wheelbarrows. The company loaned a team and grader. Soon the desert growth vanished, and the fairways were bordered with windrows of stones.

Grass greens were out of the question, as irrigation water could not be brought to the uneven terrain. The greens for this skin course were made by leveling a circular piece of ground about thirty feet in diameter and covering it with sand impregnated with a light oil. At each green was a wooden instrument made of a two-foot length of one-by-four board with a handle attached. This was used to smooth paths from the ball to the cup, thus filling up footprints and other irregularities.

The tees were slabs of concrete about five by ten feet dimension, with sections of rubber belting imbedded at the ends. Boxes of wet sand were provided for the molding of tees to support the balls.

The company built a small clubhouse and the Verde Valley Golf

Club was in business. Special course rules were devised, such as making it permissible to move a ball in the rough when it was in a bush, a clump of prickly pear, a badger hole or against a rock. Players got used to the vanishing ball; if one hit a rock in the rough or on the fairway, where large rocks might still be imbedded, it would simply disappear in the air or the desert flora and might never be seen again.

Play got under way in 1915. To belong to the club found a growing acceptance, though there still were those who wouldn't be caught dead with sticks in their hands.

Brave men led the way to the donning of plus four pants, and soon nearly all the male club members were enduring the jibes of those who had put away childish things.

A popular set of clubs was a brassie, a spoon, a mid iron, a mashie and a putter. Those who wanted to put on dog might add a driving iron, a cleek, a jigger and a niblick. All shafts were of hickory, and the mortality of those wooden sticks was ghastly, as if one took a divot he would probably lift or scar a rock and shatter the shaft. The edges of all club heads were battered and ragged.

The ladies formed their own groups and the bold ones wore skirts almost half way to the knees. New friendships were made, old ones broken—as when in a foursome one lady demanded the right to use a club to make a furrow through the sand from the ball to the cup to guide the course of the pellet. The game was ended, the foursome was disbanded, and the friendships were shot all to hell.

The skin course had been used for seven years when Charles W. Clark, a golfer himself, authorized the expenditure of $50,000 for a new golfing layout. Irrigated ranch lands around Peck's Lake were appropriated, together with some high ground to which water was pumped from the lake. The McLaren brothers, Alex and Jock, professional golf architects were employed in 1922, and a new nine-hole grass course came into being. Greens were of matted and rolled cottonseed hulls. Also erected were a fine clubhouse, a caddy house and a greenskeeper's residence. A spacious dance hall was built at the edge of the lake close by.

The new golf course was ready for use in 1924. The club members were proud to call it the sportiest course in Arizona, traveling as it did over hill and dale, and twice across the lake at tees two and eight. These holes were abominations for the neophytes, and they weren't always so good for the more experienced golfers, either. No. 2 could be endured, as one had a hill to shoot off of, and the carry was only about a hundred yards. But that No. 8! It came to be called by a variety of names: "the Horrible Eight," "the Slough of Despond," "the Terror of Peck's Lake," and, more commonly and more simply, "that S.O.B." With a carry of a hundred and fifty yards and the tee at lake level, the water became a graveyard for hundreds of balls. The club pro laid in a supply of floaters, and on days of heavy play a boy in a row boat stood by to retrieve, for a fee, the balls that did not make it across.

No. 8 became so unpopular that the tee was moved to a point halfway across the causeway bridging the lake at that point. The ladies' tees on both water holes were on the greens side of the water.

The Verde Valley Golf Club celebrated its first full year of play by entertaining the Arizona State Golf Association at its annual tournament in the fall of 1925. Again in 1929 the state tournament was held at the Verde Valley Club, its members lured by the lavish entertainment which the club and the United Verde provided. But a nine-hole course did not have the capacity to handle the growing membership of the state association, and no more tournaments of such scope were held in the Verde Valley.

Under the name of the Verde Valley Country Club the course has remained in active use, though it now has no financial support except from its membership.

Boating and boat racing were at one time popular sports at Peck's Lake, where the United Verde Copper Company provided and equipped playgrounds for the public. Concrete tennis courts were built at both Jerome and Clarkdale.

After the fine $125,000 Clark Memorial Club that had been built for the people of Clarkdale in accordance with a bequest in Senator Clark's will had been opened in 1927, United Verde employees at Jerome requested similar facilities. The big four story new hospital at Jerome was placed in service in the same year the old hospital at Jerome was converted into a clubhouse. A swimming pool was part of the Clarkdale club; a swimming pool was built on the 300 surface level at Jerome. A clubhouse with swimming pool was built in the Mexican quarter at Clarkdale; the Jerome Mexicans requested equal treatment. So a club house with swimming pool was built in Jerome's foreign quarter; the United Verde Extension donated the ground.

Jerome had its poker clubs for the men and bridge clubs for the women. The many types of gambling games in play before the law closed them are mentioned in chapters 12 and 15 of this book.

Two ancient sports were enjoyed by Jerome residents from the camp's first days—hunting and fishing. The mountains and vales of Yavapai County furnished some of the finest hunting grounds in the West. Deer and antelope abounded, and there were bear and mountain lion too. Quail and rabbit were abundant; wild turkey gobbled in the forests. Elk were imported. The several permanent streams provided fine fishing. The sportsman could choose his game and find it with the aid of saddle- and pack-horses. There were but few roads leading to the game country in the early days.

Jerome was hungry for culture, and organized drama clubs and opera groups. It had some good talent, dramatic, voice, and musical, for the production of plays and operas. No sooner had Clark's Masonic building been completed in 1900 than Walter Miller began booking theatrical and musical troupes that Jerome might enjoy talent such as other cities were favored with. The third floor of the building was designed as an opera house which would seat several hundred people. Following is part of an announcement in *The Jerome Mining News* showing some of the bookings for the fall season of 1900:

"At the opera house on October 16 Finnegan's ball will appear, with Murray and Mack. On October 22, Uncle Tom's Cabin.

"On October 30, Ten Nights in a Bar Room, a play which everywhere has proven a sensation unparalleled in the history of the drama. The sobs and tears of sympathy from audiences of all sexes and ages, who come to witness this true picture, are evidences of its wonderful dramatic power. . . . Heads of families, members of churches, all interested in the propagation of the great principles of temperance, have borne testimony to the lifelike delineation of folly, misery, madness and crime caused by the brutal, disgusting, and demoralizing vice of drunkenness."

. Bill Adams didn't permit this boost for temperance to dominate the column in which it appeared. Directly above the notice of opera house events appeared the advertisement of J. P. Taggart's liquor store on Main Street.

The traveling troupes of actors became fewer and fewer as the motion picture shows invaded the camp and began to furnish entertainment at a minimum price. The first "theaters" were vacant storerooms and basements. Ralph Smith opened his nickelodeon in 1906, soon to be followed by Clark's Electric Theater. Others followed: The Zaragosa of Santiago Tisnado, the Coliseum by Billy Haskins, the Lyric by the Johnston Brothers, the Liberty by Phil Pecharich. There was a Ritz, too, of course.

Thus were the people of Jerome in their eyrie able to thrill and laugh and cry, about as soon as those in more accessible and populous areas, to the mimes of the best known expositors of a fledgling art—such as Norma Talmadge, Dorothy Gish, Lila Lee, Theda Bara, Pearl White, William Farnum, John Barrymore, Tom Mix, Harold Lloyd and Fatty Arbuckle.

There was no place in or near Jerome where a circus could be staged, but the people of the camp were not to be denied the opportunity to see such shows. They were brought to Jerome Junction, where there was plenty of open, level ground, and excursion trains were run from Jerome, Prescott and Ash Fork to the performances.

Hoover and Cordiner had a stage in their Fashion Saloon, and booked their own favored brand of entertainment. Other saloons provided entertainers also.

Educational as well as recreational was the Jerome public library. A group of women dedicated to Jerome's cultural advancement were responsible for the founding of the library in the early 'twenties. Chief among the women was Mrs. H. J. (Annie) Minhinnick, who became the librarian and devoted years of her life to this institution which grew from a few books to more than 16,000. Donations from citizens, merchants, business and professional men, clubs, lodges, the United Verde and United Verde Extension companies aided in the library's rapid growth. Starting in a small room downtown, it was moved to the clubhouse (the old hospital) in 1928. Annie Minhinnick continued as librarian until her death in 1947.

There were some surreptitious activities, too. For instance, rumor, if pursued energetically enough, might lead one to a cockfight. Then there were badger fighting and snipe hunting, engaged in purely for the purpose of educating the tenderfoot. If he emerged from one of those experiences with his temper unruffled and his sense of humor undamaged, he was ready to be recognized as a true citizen of the West.

The camp laughed for days at the outcome of one such alleged educational effort. A real tenderfoot in the camp was the especial guest at a badger fight, hosted by two Jerome jokesters. After a few weeks these same men talked the youngster into agreeing to a snipe hunt down at Peck's Lake. Happy in the expectation that they were pulling an unusual coup they had no suspicion that the young man's education was farther along than they knew.

So on a fine spring evening the jokesters and their one time victim drove down to the lake. At dusk the young man was stationed with a lantern and a gunny sack at the edge of a tule marsh. He was told by his two companions that they would set their traps farther back on the trail. Instead, they went up to Connor and Ettinger's cigar store in Clarkdale to tell the boys there of their clever double coup.

For some reason no one laughed. Hadn't the young man, the listeners asked, been a good sport? Hadn't he taken his medicine like a man, with no griping? So just why did he rate being taken in a second time?

Discomfited, the two men drove back to the lake, lit their lanterns, and went up the trail to where they had left their intended victim. He was gone, and to their horror they found a smashed lantern, a torn coat, and a hat floating in the water at the edge of the marsh. They shouted the young man's name. They scouted the nearby bushes. They waded among the tules. They did not find the body.

Badly frightened the pair went back to town to find Jim Roberts, then deputy sheriff at Clarkdale. Entering the cigar store, they received a humiliating shock.

Sitting on a stool, grinning happily at them, was the youngster who had been a tenderfoot but was a tenderfoot no longer. Those in the place who were not matching his grin were laughing out loud.

18

Where They Slept

In writing articles describing enterprises or buildings which were a credit to Jerome, editor Bill Adams invariably resorted to the use of superlatives. He went all out in describing some of Jerome's earlier hotels.

The Montana Hotel (1900) was a magnificent structure, in the building of which "Croesus with all his wealth could not have done more." And, "people were drawn to it by the irresistible impression of grandeur and comfort."

The new Bartlett Hotel (1901) was "one of the finest hostelries on the Pacific Coast, perfect in every detail."

Adams wasn't editor of the *Jerome News* anymore when the big new Hotel Jerome was built in 1917, but a successor was equally boastful in describing it. *The Verde Copper News* stated that it was the "most attractive, the most modern, most comfortable and most nearly fire-proof hotel in northern Arizona." It marked, the paper said, the transition of Jerome from a mining camp to a city.

In its day Jerome had dozens of houses to accommodate roomers, but only a few which were built with the comfort and safety of the occupants particularly in mind. At the beginning of copper production the United Verde had its own rooming and boarding houses up above the mine, but when the demands for space for the new smelter in 1894 took these away William A. Clark began to plan for a hotel to accommodate his employees close by the plant.

Meanwhile downtown, on the spot where the ruins of the Bartlett now stand, the Grand View Hotel, the first two story building in Jerome, was built by Samuel F. Meguire and was acclaimed the valley's finest. It had a room large enough for dances, and thus became the entertainment center of Jerome. "All the elite and gayety of Jerome were there to trip their light fantastic feet," editor Wilcox of *The Jerome*

Chronicle wrote of an 1895 dance at the Grand View. "The lythe and gayety of Jerome were upon the floor, floating away like a wind blown feather. . . ."

The Grand View was consumed in the 1897 fire, and rebuilt only to be lost in the fire of 1898. That finished Meguire's building on Main Street. He sold the lot to E. C. Bartlett and later built a small hotel of the same name on Hull Avenue.

Mrs. John H. Boyd was one of the earlier of the hotel operators—in fact, one of the earliest inhabitants of the Black Hills camp. She was a sister of Angus McKinnon, who in 1876 located claims, individually and with M. A. Ruffner, subsequently included in the United Verde group. Kitty Boyd first operated the St. Charles Hotel, burned in 1897. In 1898 she built the brick-walled Boyd Hotel, which still stands on Main Street.

The first hotel in Jerome of solid construction was the Connor, built of stone. After the 1897 fire it was rebuilt, using the original walls, all that was left; but after it was engulfed in the 1898 conflagration Dave Connor cleared the site and rebuilt with brick. In the 1899 fire it was gutted but the walls stood. On the lower floor was a saloon, a restaurant, and rooms for stores; the second story had twenty-three well equipped rooms for boarders and transients.

In 1899 William A. Clark commenced the construction of his huge Montana Hotel, close to the mine at the northern base of Cleopatra Hill. At the time it was opened in the spring of 1900, it was the largest, and declared to be the most ornate, hotel in Arizona. It was four stories in height, 75 by 175 feet in dimension, with pillars and balconies in front and at either end. It was built of hewn sandstone and brick. *The Jerome Mining News* said that "with its pediments, heavy rails and balusters, architraves and cornices, it presents one of the finest pieces of architecture to be found in any country." The architect and construction overseer of the hotel was F. H. Perkins, also builder of the Masonic Hall or Miller building, and called by *The Jerome Reporter* a "master builder," a genius, and a worker of great things in his line.

The interior of the Montana Hotel was surprisingly luxurious for an establishment built contiguous to a smoking smelter and intended principally for miners and smeltermen. The main dining room seated four hundred; a smaller private dining room seated forty. It housed its own butcher shop, bakery, barber shop, laundry, commissary and pantries. It had a spacious kitchen—"its culinary has three twelve-foot ranges." Its lobby was large, with a broad stairway winding upward. The dining room was "tile wainscoted, with paneled and decorated ceilings. From the center of each of these daintily decorated panels hangs a beautiful chandelier, wrought in old copper. (The room) presents a magnificently gorgeous appearance." Adams.

The Montana had two hundred bedrooms, and could sleep three hundred and fifty. An employee of the United Verde could occupy a room for five dollars a month, and take his meals at one dollar a day. Transients were taken only if they could not be accommodated downtown.

The Montana Hotel was totally destroyed by fire in 1915. The company announced to the people of Jerome that it would not rebuild if other houses could accommodate their men at reasonable rates. If they raised prices, then other quarters would be furnished its employees, the company warned.

In the passing of the Montana, Jerome lost one of its most distinctive landmarks. It loomed high above all other buildings and could be seen from far across the valley.

In 1901 the Bartlett Hotel was completed. It faced Main Street with two stories, and it had five rooms for stores on the sub-level on First Street, on the incline down to Hull Avenue. Its builder was E. C. Bartlett, a Tucson businessman.

The interior was lavishly furnished and decorated, according to the *News*. The guest rooms "cannot be excelled by any hotel on the Pacific Coast, in size or in the manner of their furnishings." Each room was decorated in a different color and had lace curtains at the windows. *The News* had its printing plant and office in the Bartlett for twenty years.

The Bartlett was one of the buildings affected by moving ground several decades after it was built; there was cracking of the brick walls, and due to the danger of falling masonry the upper floor was removed, leaving the picturesque arched ruin which thousands of people have photographed and sketched.

The Leland Hotel was built following the second big fire at First Street and Hull Avenue, across the street and below the Bartlett. It was a two-story frame structure. It was in this hotel that the 1899 fire started.

BRENNAN PHOTO

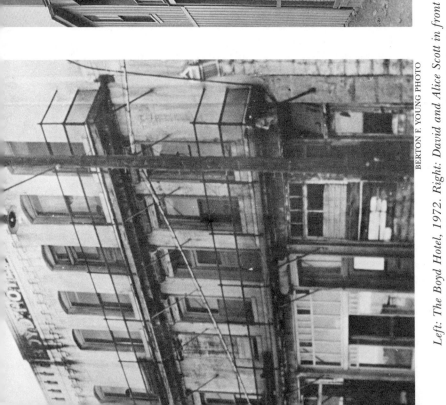

BERTON F. YOUNG PHOTO

Left: The Boyd Hotel, 1972. Right: David and Alice Scott in front of the Mountain View Boarding House, operated by Mrs. Muhler, circa 1910. (Jerome Historical Society, Willard Col.)

Also destroyed in this fire was the Ryan Hotel on Hull Avenue, another two-story frame structure.

All over central Jerome were rooming and apartment houses of small size.

The largest hotel downtown Jerome was to know was the Hotel Jerome, built in 1917. Pioneer Rudolph Rothermel and his son-in-law Harry Parker built it. This reinforced concrete structure was four stories high at street level on Hull Avenue, plus two stories on the steep slope below.

The hotel had sixty rooms for guests on the upper three floors. It boasted an elevator, the first passenger lift in Jerome. Half the rooms had private baths, and each room had hot and cold running water and steam heat. It had a spacious lobby, a large dining room, a laundry and barber shop.

The Hotel Jerome had a successful existence until the depression years and the long shutdown of the mine and smelter; then it was closed. During World War II, when copper production was stepped up and miners were shipped in from Michigan, it was used to house these men. Now, though only an empty shell, its six-story rear elevation is still an impressive sight as Jerome is approached from the east.

The large United Verde apartment house on Clark Street was built in 1918. It still stands in fair form. It contains thirty-two three- and four-room apartments.

One of the most attractive hotels in the Jerome area was the Daisy, built by James S. Douglas in 1918 above the United Verde Extension mine. Constructed of stuccoed cement block with many arches and a tile roof, it stood out boldly on the slope of the hill. It had forty rooms, a fine billiard and pool room, a spacious dining room and a finely equipped kitchen. After operating for awhile under company management, at a loss, it was leased to Sam Lee, who operated it until the United Verde Extension properties ceased production. Vandals partially wrecked the interior of the hotel prior to its being turned over to salvagers. What is left of the building is a roofless empty shell, but a picturesque one, its multiple arches attracting a host of photographers and artists of pen and brush.

When the United Verde built a new hospital in 1917 it converted the older four story structure into a dormitory for its employees, naming it the Hampton House for the mining claim on which it was built.

Above: The Hotel Jerome as it appeared when completed in 1917.
Below: The Bartlett Hotel in 1919. (Jerome Historical Society)

Another hotel operated in the first two decades of the century was the Mountain View House, located at the foot of Main Street hill and East Avenue, the Hogback road. It was owned and operated by Mrs. Melena Metzler, mother of Mrs. A. K. (Laura) Williams, long active in Jerome affairs and secretary-treasurer of the Jerome Historical Society since its organization. It has long since been dismantled.

Near the center of town was the Central Hotel, built by Frank DeZolt in Jerome boom days. In 1924 it was sold to Joe Revello. At this writing it is owned and occupied by Dr. and Mrs. O. L. Hiett.

One of the older structures was the Sullivan Hotel on North Main Street in the north business block. It was operated by John Sullivan, father of John L. Sullivan, one of the state's early attorney generals. Its upper story removed, it is still owned by members of the family, who operate tourist shops.

Well known apartment houses of Jerome were the Sullivan, the Haskins, and the Reese buildings. These still stand. There were dozens of smaller lodging houses during Jerome's busiest days, nearly all of which have disappeared. These included Charles Rucker's Black House, where one could sleep for twenty-five cents a night.

The United Verde & Pacific Railway owned the Junction Hotel at Jerome Junction, which was operated under lease from 1894 to 1920. It supplied lodging and meals to the considerable number of men who worked at transferring freight from the broad gauge to the narrow gauge cars destined for Jerome.

In Jerome's most crowded days there were not nearly enough beds to supply the demand. Some of the rooming houses relieved the situation by placing extra cots in a room and sleeping their tenants in shifts, in conformity with the working hours of the men in the mines. Thus one room could sleep six men or more!

Schools and Churches

The Schools

When William A. Clark took over the United Verde and began to smelt copper, enough families with children came to Jerome to require the services of a school teacher. First one room was enough; but in 1895 the enrollment had increased to sixty-four, and a two-room school was provided. Ida Williams was the only teacher until the following year, when a second school marm was hired. These were the forerunners of the many hundreds of teachers, men and women, who served Jerome's schools through the years.

By 1905 the enrollment had expanded to 218, with six teachers employed. A two-story frame school building had been erected, and in that year a three-year high school course had been added to the curriculum. Professor B. R. Scudder was superintendent. He held this post until 1908, when he resigned and Professor C. O. Case was employed. The enrollment had then increased to 265. Case held the superintendency until early 1912, when he successfully sought the office of Superintendent of Education of the new state of Arizona. A. L. Lackey served temporarily until the fall of 1912 when Professor R. G. Stevenson took the office, which he held until 1918.

The frame school building became overcrowded, so a new building was erected, known as the high school. There were only 22 high school students, but the school board had their eyes on the future. In 1911 the first high school class was graduated—two girls. The commencement was quite an affair. The auditorium of the new building wasn't ready for occupancy, so the opera house was engaged. Wilmith Case was valedictorian, Ruth Fallon the salutatorian. The Honorable Henry F. Ashurst of Flagstaff, an orator of note who subsequently was to be one of the most fervid voices in the United States Senate, delivered the commencement address.

In 1914 Jerome's schools enrolled 329 pupils, 19 of them in the high school. In the spring of 1915 three of these graduated: Helen

The only school buildings left in Jerome, all abandoned. Above: The Clark Street "grammar" school.

Below: The Mingus high school group of buildings, with a distance view of the Verde River basin and the rising mountain lands beyond.

Thorbeck, Pearl Priestly, and Ersel Garrison. The commencement exercises were the first to be held in the new auditorium.

Enrollment passed 500 in 1915. The inflow of children of school age was so rapid, coincidently with the mining boom, that in 1919 more than 1000 students were attending Jerome's schools. In 1917 a new primary school was built on Main Street, at the head of the steep hill leading down to the Hogback, but that became inadequate almost immediately. Adjacent to the lower level of the building seven frame class rooms were erected; then the auditorium was divided into four more rooms. The teaching staff had increased to fifty, nine of them high school instructors.

Still more space was needed, so in 1920 another primary school was built in Deception Gulch. In 1924 a contract was let for an up-to-date building on the site of the original primary school. In 1923 the fine high school plant on the Hogback was completed, designed to accommodate up to 500 students.

John Oscar Mullen became school superintendent in 1918 and served in that post until 1947. His goals had been two; to make the Jerome school system one of the finest in the Southwest, and to build a new high school plant worthy of the system and the town. Both goals were reached.

J. O. Mullen loomed large among Arizona's educators. He retired in failing health, and died in 1954 at age 75.

Contiguous to the new high school buildings on the Hogback the United Verde Extension Mining Company had erected a two-story, $75,000 building planned as a hospital but never put to use. In 1929 this building was presented to the school district, and was remodeled for school purposes.

Among the graduates of the 1926 class of the Jerome high school was Lewis J. McDonald, who upon his graduation from Arizona State College at Flagstaff became principal of the Jerome high school. Upon Mullen's retirement McDonald became superintendent, then went on to an important post with his alma mater, later to become Northern Arizona University.

In the ten years prior to 1928 school enrollment more than doubled. In that year enrollment was 1,529; 1,234 elementary, 148 junior high, and 147 high school. The school board was then operating four schools.

SCHOOLS AND CHURCHES

The three primary schools taught grades one to six, the high school grades seven to twelve.

As this is written there are no schools operating in Jerome. The few children below high school age are bussed to Clarkdale, for after the closing of the mines in 1953 the Jerome and Clarkdale districts consolidated. Subsequently the Mingus Union High School district was formed, taking in all the upper Verde Valley school districts. The Jerome high school was then put to use for the union district, but has been abandoned for a modern school plant at Cottonwood.

The Main Street and Walnut Gulch buildings have been dismantled. The Clark Street structure has become the property of the town. The high school plant, a group of buildings that could not be replaced for less than two million dollars, stands silent, occupied only by the ghosts of a seething past and a shattered present.

The Churches

Jerome had four churches at the turn of the century. The first house of worship in the town was erected by the Baptists in 1896 on the hill road leading to the smelter. This building escaped the big fires. When the United Verde hospital on Main Street was burned in 1898, and while a new brick structure was being built, the Baptist church was used as a hospital. Clarence E. Wager tells of this in his memoirs, and states that the pews were used as emergency beds.

The Baptists lacked sufficient members and funds to maintain a church, and in 1899 the building was sold to the Congregational Church, which started its service to Jerome under the pastorate of Rev. E. H. Ashmun. They supported their organization until 1912, when they found the burden of maintaining a building and paying a pastor too great. They sold the building to the Episcopal Church and disbanded.

The Catholics followed the Congregationalists in erecting a church building in 1896—a frame building on Giroux Street. There was a substantial number of Catholics in Jerome, that religion predominating among the Mexicans, and being in considerable strength in the European group. Jerome was placed in the Prescott diocese, and was visited regularly by Fr. Quetu of that city; and it was under his guidance that the brick structure which stands today was erected in 1899 and 1900 after the original building was destroyed in the 1898

135

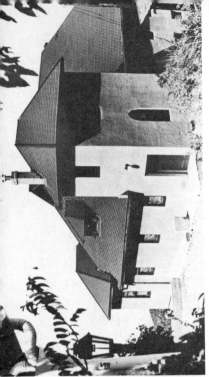

Jerome's remaining church structures as they appear today. Above, left, the Holy Family Catholic Church, Bob Bradshaw photo. Above, right, the Haven Methodist Church, George Kennedy photo. Below, left, Christ Episcopal Church, and right, the "powder box" church, Herb Young photos.

fire. This church was served by a Prescott priest until the Jerome parish was established in 1908. Fr. Rene O. Rampont became the first priest in residence; one of his main duties was to liquidate the $5,000 debt which hovered over the $20,000 building. That duty had been discharged when Rampont returned to his native France in 1914 to join the French forces in the war with Germany.

The Jerome Catholic Church has never been without a resident priest since 1908.

The Methodist group organized in 1900 with 25 members, and Rev. George M. Smith was appointed pastor. With $2,000 raised and promised, they built a small church at the corner of School Street and Center Avenue, together with a small parsonage. This served until the needs of an expanding congregation in Jerome's most prosperous decade inspired the building of a new $15,000 church in 1927, near the old one which was sold and remodeled into apartments. Haven United Methodist Church, still alive, shares a pastorate with the United Methodist Church of Clarkdale.

An Episcopal Church also was organized in 1900, with Rev. E. G. Lee the priest in charge. It held its meetings in the Masonic Hall or in the opera house until the Congregational Church building became theirs. This building fell victim to ground movement and was condemned and demolished in 1926. The Episcopalians then built, in 1927, an attractive new house of worship on Clark Street near the town's center. This served the church until the mine shut-down in 1953, when it was closed and its furnishings and stained glass windows moved away. The shell of this building is now owned by the Jerome Historical Society, which has included it in its renovation program covering the historic buildings of Jerome.

Seeds of other churches sprouted in Jerome, but did not flourish. The Salvation Army was active in the early years. The Christian Science Church had a following. In 1925 the African Methodist Episcopal Zion Church was organized in Jerome, using the basement of Haven Church for its services. It did not last long.

Though it took shape in a later period than this book is planned to cover, mention may be made of another church, its building constructed in the late thirties, which has been featured as one of Jerome's unique landmarks. It was constructed on a prominence above the road leading from the Hogback to the Douglas mansion, now a State Histor-

137

ical Museum. It was and still is called "the powder box church," because it was supposed to have been constructed of empty boxes which had contained dynamite used at the mine. The materials of construction were actually empty government ammunition boxes and lumber donated by the United Verde and United Verde Extension and salvaged from dismantled buildings. The structure was built by members of the Mexican Methodist Church, the leader of whom was Sabino Gonzales, a Jerome barber. He was also the architect, and much of the labor of erecting the structure was performed by him. It was truly a labor of love and a notable achievement for this small band of churchmen. It stands vacant now.

Few churches ever have it easy. The going may be especially difficult in a community where people of low income are in the majority, and where dependence is on one industry which at times may close down. Jerome's little churches at times were hard put to keep going; in such cases the poor pastors were apt to feel the hard times most. A story told as true by one who lived in Jerome in the early days illustrates the plight of one pastor and the direct action he took to relieve a shortage. Without coal or wood for the church and parsonage he armed himself with an axe and attacked the empty fuel shed. By the time he had demolished and burned the planking of the coal bin inside the shed the members of the church woke up and fuel was delivered.

The fact that the Jerome churches survived through all vicissitudes for more than fifty years speaks well for the dedication of the comparatively small groups of men and women who worked hard to keep them going.

Group posing after First Communion at the Holy Family Catholic Church in 1947. Photograph by the Shen Studio (Jerome Historical Society, Shen Col.)

They Called Them "Characters"

In every community will be found some individuals whose personalities or acts set them apart from the normal run of citizens. Of these Jerome had its share.

In my interviews with old timers over a period of more than half a century there was a notable recurrence of the names of certain men who, while they took no particular part in the development of Jerome, made good conversation pieces—the type of character about whom people liked to gossip, or laugh, or perhaps even shed a tear or two.

So, to show a side of Jerome not previously touched upon, I give here sketches of a few of these characters as told by narrators of an earlier day. (Look to the Appendix for information on Jerome's business and professional men and women.)

"Handsome Dan" Murphy

He was called "handsome" mainly because he wasn't. What he lacked in looks he made up in aggressiveness, and as a colorful character and man about town he had few equals.

He had led a seamy life, which started with an incident in his hometown of Boston, where his family was prominent and prosperous. When he was thirteen years of age he decided he was old enough to indulge in manly habits, so he bought a pipe and a package of tobacco, lit up, and strolled down the street. Fortuitously he encountered his parish priest who, horrified that one of his choir boys should engage in the sinful habit of smoking, knocked the pipe from Dan's mouth. Dan's response was to strike a blow that laid the priest flat on his back. For this he was sent to reform school; after that his family bought him a ticket West and told him that thenceforth he would have to shift for himself.

After wandering awhile among the Western mining camps he landed in Jerome. Bob Tally was then mine superintendent; he had known Dan in Butte, and took a liking to this fellow Irishman. He saw that he had work. He helped straighten out things after some of Dan's weekend belligerent sprees, and saw that he wasn't penalized too severely if he took an extra day or two off to recover.

When the United Verde changed hands the new management was less tolerant of men who periodically failed to report to work because of drunkenness, and Dan found himself out of a job. He did odd jobs until he found himself physically unable to do a day's work, then he managed with friends' help to get admitted to the Pioneers' Home at Prescott. When it was discovered that he was smuggling liquor into the home and sharing it with other inmates, he was expelled.

Back in Jerome, broken in health, he lived for awhile on handouts. He occupied a poor room in a small hotel; when acquaintances reported to the police that he had not been seen for two or three days, deputy Tom Cantrell investigated. He found Dan's body under a piece of furniture.

A brother had Dan's body returned by air express to Boston, where at last he was permitted to join others of his family in their cemetery plot.

Box Car Riley

Another man of neglected achievement potential, Box Car Riley—his Christian name seems to have been forgotten—became a subject of gossip because of characteristics which stemmed not from his intellect.

He was a native of Ireland, of a well-to-do family, though as a second son he was not in line for substantial inheritance. But he was given a good education; he graduated from the University of Dublin with BA and LLB degrees. But he developed into a ne'er-do-well, and that he might not tarnish his family's honor he was bundled off to America, in the hope that if forced to shift for himself in a new land he might make something of himself.

What he made of himself could not have pleased his family.

He was working as a laborer in an open pit mine in Nevada when E. E. Vanderhoef, under whom Riley was working, was offered the superintendency of the pit operation at Jerome. He brought Riley with him. He picked up the name "Box Car" during his work in maintenance of railroad track on the pit benches.

On weekends he would travel high and wide, usually in company with his bosom friend Handsome Dan Murphy. After communing with the bottle his thoughts would revert to the past and he would give extensive recitations from the Bible or from whichever of Shakespeare's plays came to mind. He was equally eloquent in his rendition of Portia, Brutus or Caliban. Additional contributions of liquor would keep the show going indefinitely. The next day he would be back on the job as usual, having great power of recovery.

Box Car Riley died shortly after pit stripping was discontinued in 1940.

Elderberry Bill

He always stood straight and tall, head up and shoulders back. At first sight you would never have pinned the tag "pathetic" on William Cowan. Yet pathetic I and others found him; it was sad to observe a man longing so intensely for things he could never have.

Bill came from a well-to-do Massachusetts family. In his youth he spent considerable time sailing and riding, and attending college, where Charles W. Clark became acquainted with him. His life was changed when he suffered a head injury in a riding accident. In a trephining operation a portion of his skull was removed and a silver plate inserted. He was mentally never the same again.

He wandered West. He was clerking at the Denver Athletic Club when visiting Charlie Clark recognized him. Cowan sought of him and obtained a job at the United Verde. After serving the desk at the Montana Hotel for a while he was given a timekeeping job.

While at the hotel, before dinner each evening Bill attired himself in a swallow-tail coat, striped trousers and a wing collar. He wore a vandyke beard. He seemed oblivious to the smiles or sneers and quips of the other men of the camp. Because of his distinguished appearance some of the young men named him "the Duke"—or "the Count," which inevitably became "the Count of No Account."

After dinner he would go down the hill to the Fashion. He never drank, as alcohol brought pain to his damaged head, but he spent much time at the slot machines, laughing like a child when he made a win, walking disconsolately away when all his nickels were gone.

He got his most common name, "Elderberry Bill," from his gathering of elderberries from the mountainside when they had ripened, bringing full pails of them to those who were friendly to him.

When he first came to Jerome he tried to establish himself with the social set. He attended dances. He purchased full dress apparel and appeared in splendor. But the single women always seemed to have full cards. He was deeply hurt, and returned his suit to the tailor and ordered it sold.

His happy moods were so rare as to be almost non-existent. Only two do I recall now. A visiting artist, interested in Bill as a model for sketches, made some which he presented to Cowan. One showed the landscape features of the famous painting "September Morn," but the nude figure in the foreground was not a female, but Bill, without clothes except for the soft, wide-brimmed Stetson he was seldom without, and in the same crouching pose as the original. Bill laughed about that, and was so pleased he had copies made to distribute to those he called friends.

During the depression he began to show signs of mental deterioration. He was given light physical work at the Clarkdale smelter. It was during this period that I saw Bill happy again, but, sadly, only briefly. A friendly Christmas card from an old-time lady friend sent him hurrying to Chicago with the hope, as he intimated to me, that at last he would find a mate. He was gone no more than ten days, and returned in such a confused state of mind that he sought my help, through the station agent, in finding his way to his room at the company dormitory.

What happened in Chicago Bill would not say, but the shock was damaging to his already failing mentality. Soon afterward he was sent to the state mental hospital at Phoenix, where he found an interest in tending flowers in the hospital yard. He died there in 1933.

The Seventh Earl

The people of Jerome didn't know until he died in 1914 that their district had harbored a titled Scotsman for a number of years. They knew John Sinclair as a friendly man who perhaps once a week rode horseback into town from the Copper Chief mine south of Jerome where he was employed as a mining engineer. His bearded face became familiar to many in Jerome.

John Sinclair was the seventeenth Earl of Caithness, of County Caithness, at the northern jut of Scotland. The property of the ancient earldom once had been extensive, but over the centuries had become entailed and had dwindled to a small estate. Sinclair abandoned his title and came to America where he successfully sought his fortune as a mining engineer.

He retired to Los Angeles, where he became known as a patron of good works.

The Mad Russian

That's what the old timers called him; none of them knew his real name. Burly, bearded and jovial, he was thought to be a geologist making undercover investigations for some mining firm. It was rumored that he had a Russian title. He lived out in the hills somewhere, and periodically he would come riding into town horseback, accompanied by a lackey.

He received frequent and sizeable Russian gourmet items. About once a month he would break out cases of vodka and caviar and throw a party, to which everyone was invited. Once when Senator Clark was in town he laid out a particularly sumptuous spread in honor of the Senator, he said. But Clark had another engagement, was the word.

He gained the name of "the mad Russian" because of his boisterous parties and his perpetual discourses on the fabulous wealth beneath and surrounding Jerome, its real potential as yet unscratched. When he left Jerome he left that tag behind.

White the Hermit

When his shack on the southern edge of Jerome burned down in 1929, it was reported in *The Verde Copper News* as having belonged to Frank White. Others knew him as either Charlie or Bill White.

He came to Jerome from Tombstone in the camp's young days. He was a loner. He built his shack himself of scrap salvaged from here and there. He was away when it burned; he lost all his possessions, including some rare books.

He was a scholar, and could quote from the scriptures and the classics. He was better known as a spiritualist, and many stories were told of his having been heard carrying on conversations with sojourners from another world.

While he was physically able he cut firewood in the surrounding hills and packed it into town on a pair of burros, selling it to the residents. After the loss of his possessions he burrowed out a little cavern under the overhanging sidewalk leading down to the Hogback. When failing strength compelled him to abandon woodcutting, he took to peddling small items on the streets or from door to door. He refused all offers of charity.

When he died a nephew from New York claimed the remains.

Bob Winchester

In asking the real old timers which of the early day "characters" he best remembered, usually one of the first mentioned would be Bob Winchester.

He was one of the group who loved a fight, and it needed small excuse to set his fists swinging. He worked at the smelter.

Once Doc Woods told him that pneumonia was the cause of those bad pains in his chest and he ordered him to bed in one of the wards. Bob didn't like confinement of any kind. In the middle of the night he got thirsty and hungry, and still in his hospital gown he hurried to a nearby saloon and got a pint, then went to a restaurant. He started a quarrel with the Chinese operator, who staved off an attack by driving a carving knife through Bob's side. He was taken back to the hospital and in a few days was ready for another adventure.

A favorite story about Winchester involved a young artist and a barber. The artist was lettering a sign in a barber shop when Winchester came in for a shave. He fell fast asleep in the chair. The artist saw in the smooth, bald pate of the slumbering man an ideal ground for brush work; he painted upon Bob's shining dome the image of a huge tarantula.

Winchester next went to a restaurant and gave a waitress his order. As she returned with the food her customer removed his hat, and the girl found herself looking down upon the repulsive likeness of the giant spider. With a wild scream, which brought men running in from the street, she convulsively sent flying the tray and the food upon it.

Viewing Bob's dome, the customers roared with laughter. Bob roared with rage, returned to the barber shop and did a thorough job of wrecking it. Bob went to jail and was assessed the cost of repairs to the barber shop.

Once when he was belligerently drunk Jim Roberts locked Bob in a cell and continued his rounds. After a few bellowed threats the prisoner lighted a match and set fire to the mattress on his bunk. The smoke brought men running; Harry Crain grabbed a double jack and smashed the lock on the cell door. Bob emerged, coughing, gurgling, and gasping, but with a wicked grin on his face. He was charged with arson and got a jail term for that.

When George Mitchell, who had been the United Verde's smelter superintendent before Tom Taylor's day, went to Cananea, Sonora, to take charge of the smelter there, Winchester followed. James S. Douglas was appointed general manager; when he arrived he was given a reception at which Bob appeared, took the floor, and delivered an eloquent oration the substance of which was that young Douglas would succeed in his new role only if willing to follow the precepts of experienced men such as he and recognized the needs and rights of the working man, the real source of wealth.

It was said in Jerome that the Mexican officials found Bob Winchester too hard to cope with and shipped him back to Arizona.

Rene Rampont, S. J.   Perhaps it may seem a little out of place to include a man of the cloth in this group of "characters." Yet Father Rampont would not have minded. He was a friend of and associated with most of those named here, and his activities, some of which were rather unusual for a priest, were such as to cause him to be a much talked of man. So we'll finish this group of stories with his.

As indicated, Father Rampont was not "as a priest, a part of mere church furniture." He did not hesitate to enter a saloon; he played poker with the boys; he speculated in mining stocks and bought and sold real estate; he was a candidate for a political office.

He had studied for the priesthood in his native France. He was called to Arizona; he served the church for a time in Globe, then when Jerome was separated from the Prescott parish and a new parish established in the mining camp Rampont was appointed its first priest in May 1906. One of the reasons for the Jerome assignment was that Rampont had already established a reputation as a money raiser, and the Jerome church was in debt for more than $5,000. The debt had been discharged when the first world war sent the priest back to France in 1914. There he joined the French forces as an ambulance driver, and was in the thick of the action at the battle of Verdun. Illness forced his retirement; he returned to Jerome in 1916. The Jerome parish then had another priest.

Rampont had been successful in real estate dealings, and owned several houses in Jerome. He had bought 1000 shares of United Verde Extension stock prior to his trip to France; it made him a rich man.

The story goes that the church, frowning upon such activities, demanded that Rampont turn his possessions over to the church. This he would not do. He continued his business dealings. He was a candidate for justice of the peace, but lost. He participated in the IWW deportation in 1917, and during these and other labor troubles, was appointed a deputy sheriff and served as a watchman.

He retired from the church and went to California, where he bought a mountain home. He sent for a girl he had met while in France, married her, and had children. He later fell upon evil times; he lost two children by drowning in a lake on his ranch. He lost his property, and when practically destitute and with the loss of his eyesight imminent, he chose death by his own hand.

Elderberry Bill Cowan in front of the Bank of Jerome, which was located in the Bartlett Hotel. (Jerome Historical Society)

Postscript

Evening comes early on the eastern slope of Cleopatra Hill; around four or five o'clock of an afternoon, depending upon the season, the sun has slipped behind the crest, leaving the town clothed in shadow.

Often visitors stand on the Main Street lookout where buildings once stood, view the ruins around them, and watch the shadows flow down the undulating slopes to the east. They watch while the dusk creeps slowly onward to the river, then up the incline beyond, changing to fire as the sun's rays illumine the sculptured piles on red rocks. Then these blazing eminences stand out in startling contrast to the deep shadows of the valley and of the canyons from which they rise.

Long before the fire has vanished from the loftiest of the red rock spires, lamps are being turned on in the darkening buildings of the town; then, when finally the last tints of day fade from the eastern rim of the valley, street lights flash into scattered pattern like the lamps of a Christmas tree. The wanderers have departed; the streets are empty; Jerome's long night has begun.

What a sharp contrast is this to those riotous times of an earlier day when lights blazed all night in Jerome's never closing taverns and restaurants and houses of pleasure; when miners and smeltermen poured down the hill at intervals night and day, to join in activities which made an observer wonder if there might not be truth in the widely circulated story that Jerome was the wickedest city in America.

As the closing chapters of this book were being prepared I thought more and more of those times of long ago when in summer I, with my family and friends, would set out in our primitive motor cars and brave the stony, rutty and potholed wagon road to Oak Creek. Fording that beautiful little stream we would travel on and up the old Schnebly Hill trail. That road wasn't like the present one; the final lap was up a steep and narrow incline (still seen as a scar on the mountain side) which brought us to the rim of the plateau some distance south

PHOTOGRAPH BY JOHN DEMPSEY

Above: When the mines closed Phelps Dodge sold and moved some company houses into the Verde Valley and Prescott.
Below: When the population dropped, many structures like the Arriaga house were abandoned and eventually crumbled.

of the present road's summit. There one had a most magnificent view of the Verde Valley which included far away Jerome.

One summer evening we camped on the rim and stayed the night. The smelter at Jerome was still operating and the town was bursting with activity. After darkness came, the lights of the mining camp, which had a far greater spread than now, glittered beyond the valley's black depths like a brilliant constellation. Higher up at the smelter there was a frequent pouring of molten waste, which slid down the high face of the slag dump in rivers of orange fire. The incandescence was reflected to the clouds of smoke pouring from the smelter stacks, giving them an eerie luminosity. It was a view so entrancing that only reluctantly did we seek our cots. The star-illumined night was beautifully pleasant; we reveled in the bracing breezes so far from smoke and noise, so keenly cool that blankets were sought.

At sunrise we were treated to another sight which rivalled the one which had thrilled us the night before. The red rock sculptures that dominated the landscape down to Oak Creek and onward were now seen in different lighting, the shadows hovering among them contrasting sharply with the highlights on the carved eminences. The shades in the vales and fissures were of varying tones of violet, pale or dark according to the degree of exposure. Scattered over the slopes of the hills which rose and receded behind the sculptures, and even growing in their crevices and about their bases, were beds and undulating stretches of manzanita, scrub oak, juniper, pinyon and other mountain growth, with here and there clusters of flowers—white, red, yellow and purple. Far down in the valley shreds of mist trailed along the river.

We had seen the Grand Canyon, only eighty miles to the north, and like all who had come to view it had been enthralled with the vastness of its chromatic carvings and its dizzy depths and ever changing shadows. But we were in agreement that the vistas of that wonder of the world were not more beautiful than those of the Verde Valley, whether viewed from the eastern rim above the brilliant monuments of Oak Creek or from the heights of the Black Hills on the western side.

Many times since those early days we have visited the lookouts on the Mingus trail and on the rim of the Mogollon plateau. The smelters with their discharges of fire and brimstone have been gone these many years. Though Jerome's lights are fewer than once they were, other lights flow down the valley. The view is always inspiring, night or day. It brings back memories of years of happy living among the good and unpretentious people of this mountain land, men and women who have had unsurpassed opportunities to live close to Nature and to have learned, perhaps better than most, that man by birth should and may be really free. Inevitably it brings to those who have come to know and love this valley as their own the urge to say, "We're glad this land is home."

The United Verde Extension (Little Daisy) Mine and the Douglas Mansion with Clarkdale and the United Verde Copper Company Smelter in the distance, circa 1930. (Jerome Historical Society, McMillan Col.)

Acknowledgments

Over the years many people have told me or written of their experiences in the Jerome of an earlier day, and have probed their memories for stories of people and events. Many have helped in other ways in the production of this book and GHOSTS OF CLEOPATRA HILL. Here I name them and gratefully acknowledge their contributions and aid.

Harry Amster, Col. E. M. J. Alenius, William S. Adams.

Don Barrows, Frank F. Bartlett, Katherine Bartlett, Clarence J. Beale, John Bell, Fred Boyd, Bob Bradshaw, Isabelle A. Burrows.

A. Brodie Campbell, Dollie Canady, Ruth Cantrell, Dr. Arthur C. Carlson, Elva Haskell Carroll, Charles W. Clark, Hon. William A. Clark, Will L. Clark, John P. Connolly, Richard S. Condit, Margaret Connor, John F. Cowley, Joan Shea Cowley.

Thomas Davies, Ernest Douglas, Hon. Lewis W. Douglas, Geraldine E. Duvall.

Taylor Estes, Glenallen Minty Ewell, Frank Eberdt.

Wallace F. Ferris, Wayland Ford, Ernest Fredell, Norman French.

Charles C. S. P. Gardner, Emily Olcott Garrison, Ersel Garrison, Jennie Willard Garrison, Roland L. Giroux.

James Haskins, Dr. Lee A. Hawkins, Sherman Hazeltine, Dora Heap, Shan Holt, Dave Hopkins, Katherine M. Hopkins, Lillian Hudgens, Bertha Rucker Hughes, Charles E. Hughes.

Catherine Dicus Jolly, Thomas B. Jones, H. S. Jordan, George Jordan, Walter Jordan, Will A. Jordan.

Douglas Kell, Inez Grake Kemble, Ivy Klausman, Robert Knudson, Olive Kruse, Charles R. Kuzell, George Kennedy

Raymond C. Lane, Chonita Tisnado Lawrence, Richard E. Lawrence, Martha Jacobs Leyel, Margaret Shea Lively, Mary Shea Lyons.

George E. McMillan, John E. McMillan, Ray E. Miller, Walter C. Miller, Jr., Carl E. Mills, Ivy Moser, Milber Favell Mullen, David F. Myrick.

Vivian F. Nickerson, William E. Nicoll, Elizabeth Nihell, Ike L. Nihell.

Alfred B. Peach, Dr. Joseph Pecharich, Dr. Raymond Pecharich, Phil Pecharich, Jack B. Pullen, Mrs. Jack B. Pullen.

Helen Geary Quayle.

Milt Ray, Mert Reade, Dr. Louis E. Reber, A. L. Reese, William Roberts, Charles Elmer Riley, Dan Robinson, Lester Ruffner, Dorothy Hopkins Ryan.

Iva Carrier Shaw, Charles C. Stemmer.

Robert E. Tally, Thomas Taylor, Frederick F. Thomas, Jr., Geraldine Thomas, Arthur Train, Jr.

Paul Vojnic.

Clarence E. Wager, John Donald Walsh, Dr. J. Malcolm Walsh, V. C. Wiggins, Charles D. Willard, Donald Willard, Cecelia Barker Williams, Bert Williams, Geoff Williams, Laura Metzler Williams, Robert W. Wingfield, Clarence Wombacher, Dan Wombacher, Harriet Tritle Woodman.

Lawrence L. Young, Virna M. Young, Berton F. Young, Zelia E. Young.

*   *   *

Also I acknowledge the assistance I have received, in my search for information, from the following publications and sources:

The Jerome Chronicle; The Arizona Mining News; The Jerome Mining News; The Jerome Daily News; The Jerome Reporter; The Jerome Copper Belt; The Jerome News and Copper Belt; The Jerome Sun; The Prescott Journal Miner; The Prescott Courier, and *The Arizona Republican.*

Also: *The American Mining Journal; The Mining and Scientific Press,* and *The Mining Congress Journal.*

Also: ARIZONA, THE YOUNGEST STATE, McClintock; HISTORY OF ARIZONA, Sloane; LEGISLATIVE HISTORY OF ARIZONA TERRITORY, Kelly; ROCK TO RICHES, Dunning and Peplow; PIONEER STORIES OF ARIZONA'S VERDE VALLEY, Verde Valley Pioneers Association; and the scrap books of Governor Frederick A. Tritle.

I have also received courtesies from the Museum of Northern Arizona, Flagstaff; the Sharlot Hall Historical Museum of Arizona, Prescott;

ACKNOWLEDGMENTS

the Arizona Pioneers' Historical Society, Tucson; the Fort Verde Historical Museum, Camp Verde; the Nevada State Historical Society, Reno, the New Mexico State Library, Santa Fe, the Verde Valley Artists, Inc., and the New York City Public Library. And of course I have drawn liberally on the pictorial and published records of the Jerome Historical Society.

Marguerite B. Cooley, Director of the Arizona State Department of History and Archives, has been of great help to the Jerome Historical Society and to me in supplying historical data and in assembling a library of microfilm which records all known issues of Jerome's several newspapers.

The late Charles R. Kuzell, who entered the service of the United Verde Copper Company as a metallurgist and rose to the highest office Phelps Dodge Corporation could offer in its Western operations—that of vice president and general manager—has given me valuable information and encouragement.

My son Berton F. Young, a master of the graphic arts who designed and produced GHOSTS OF CLEOPATRA HILL, has been of inestimable aid in the preparation for publication of THEY CAME TO JEROME

It has been a pleasure to work with Parker G. Sutton, Jr., and Patricia C. Cook of Phoenician Books, Inc., producers of this book. Their keen interest and patience have been sincerely appreciated.

Thanks to E. T. Carlin for his fine cover design.

HERBERT V. YOUNG

Two of the most prominent men of Jerome's early days. Left, William M. Munds, the town's first mayor; right, Dr. Myron A. Carrier.

APPENDIX A.

A Few Whom Everyone Knew

In this section we present notes on a few of the men and women of Jerome's earlier years, known for their positions, achievements or characteristics and not covered in other sections of this book or in GHOSTS OF CLEOPATRA HILL.

The Millers: T. F. Miller, whose name was given to the dominant merchandising house of Jerome and the Verde Valley, was a brother-in-law of William A. Clark. With Clark's aid the T. F. Miller Company started doing business in Jerome even before the Jerome smelter was built, and occupied the main space in the Masonic or Miller building when that four story structure was completed. Walter C. Miller, son of T. F., was made manager of the company while still in his twenties. He became active in community affairs and a leading sportsman. He married Laura Minty, daughter of General Minty. His brother Charles was a mining engineer with the United Verde; another, brother, Evans, was manager of the Clarkdale branch of the Miller company. A son, Walter Jr., lives in Phoenix.

The Mintys: General R. H. G. Minty was a Civil War hero, distinguished mainly because of his leadership of the Union forces at the battle of Shelbyville. A son Courtney managed departments of the T. F. Miller Company. The general died in 1906.

Paul Hastings: He followed General Minty as auditor of the United Verde & Pacific railway, then went on and up to become president of the Atchison, Topeka and Santa Fe Railroad Company.

Kitty Crain: As Miss Kitty Christian she came to Jerome in 1889. She married John H. Boyd in Jerome; they moved to Mayer, where he managed a mine and died in 1893. She married Harry Crain in 1898. A son Fred engaged in business in Jerome, and is still a resident of the Verde Valley, one of the oldest of living Jerome pioneers. Kitty Crain died in 1932. More about Kitty Crain and her hotels is recounted in Chapter 14.

Harry Crain: A mining engineer who came to Jerome in 1897. After his marriage to Kitty Boyd the following year he joined his wife in the management of her hotel and other properties and in real estate and mine dealings. He died in 1937.

The Shea Family: The Sheas and those who joined their clan were among the best known of Jerome citizens. They came from Ireland, nine of them, the mother, four brothers and three sisters. Dan was the older and came to be known as "King" because of his dominance in the family and in business. Brothers Matt and Tim became associated with Dan in his enterprises; brother Con was a master plumber; brother Dennis was more or less inactive. Sister Margaret married M. J. Bradley who also became a business associate, Sister Mary married Con O'Keefe, a prominent Jerome businessman. Sister Hannah lost her life in a home fire.

Dan began his career in Jerome in the early nineties as a laborer in the mines, but he soon established a saloon, Shea's Place, at "the bend" up the hill toward the mine. Next he opened a saloon downtown on Main Street. Giving up the saloon he established a general merchandising business, which became a men's furnishings-only house.

Dan made money, bought ranch and rental properties, organized the Shea Copper Company, the stock of which was active on mining exchanges during the boom. Long before his retirement Dan acquired ranch lands in California, and when the Jerome business was sold the family moved to that state.

William Munds: He came to Arizona in 1876, and became a rancher and cattleman in the Verde Valley. He established a meat market in Jerome and became prominent in civic affairs, serving as Jerome's first mayor. He was father of John Munds, who assisted in the meat market and acted as deputy sheriff in Jerome prior to his being elected county sheriff in 1898.

John P. Connolly: Born in Ireland in 1869, and took employment with the United Verde. For six years he was foreman of the roast level operations, then worked for T. F. Miller Company for four years. In 1905 he joined the staff of the D. J. Shea Company's store, of which he became manager.

J. F. Mullin: Founded the Jerome Lumber Company with W. F. Montgomery and L. W. Pugh. For many years this was the chief establishment of its kind in the Verde Valley.

Doane and Horace Merrill: Two of Jerome's earliest general merchants, coming to the camp about 1890. Doane served briefly as postmaster in 1892, and was one of the members of Jerome's first common council. They closed out their business in the century's first decade and went to Willcox, Arizona, where they engaged in the banking business.

Henry W. Lewis: Came to Jerome from Texas in 1907 to take a position in the Jerome branch of the Bank of Arizona. When Ralph Smith resigned as manager in 1910, Lewis became assistant manager under Guy Bailey. He became manager when Bailey was murdered in 1914. He served in that capacity until his death in 1924. He was succeeded by Robert K. Porter.

Robert K. Porter: He was appointed cashier of the Bank of Jerome in 1914, when A. A. McPherson left. He had worked in the parent bank at Prescott. In 1917 he left the bank to take over the grocery store of Paz & Cota, formerly the A. H. Lyons grocery. When H. W. Lewis, manager of the Jerome Branch of the Bank of Arizona, died in 1924, Porter was named manager. Later he was transferred to Prescott headquarters of the bank. Porter was married to a sister of Mrs. Robert E. Tally.

Alex Lyons: In 1895 was a clerk in the general merchandise store of Merrill Brothers. His wife operated a millinery business. Prior to 1900 with Andy Knoblock he started Lyons & Knoblock grocery; Knoblock retired in the same year, going to San Francisco, after which Alex operated the store with brother *John Lyons.* Alex Lyons died in 1912, and the store was sold to Paz & Cota. Alex was father of *Francis Lyons,* who became a well known Jerome stock and insurance broker. *Alex Lyons Jr.* was another son.

R. S. Sturmer: Operated one of Jerome's first bakeries; was member of Jerome's first town council.

Joseph Thorbeck: Operated a bakery in Jerome for many years, with aid of sons August and Hugo. German immigrant; wife died in 1906, leaving six children. He began his Jerome career as baker for Merrill Brothers in the 1890's.

Elwin F. Tarr: Operator of Jerome's first drug store in 1890's.

William Holliday: Operated one of Jerome's first livery stables, the Terrace. Married Rose Kirwagen, daughter of orchardist *John Kirwagen,* murdered at the ranch in 1902.

Ed Tovrea: Came to Jerome in 1908, founded Jerome Meat Company with Ben Clay. Born in Illinois in 1861. Was Jerome's second mayor.

He left during the first decade to operate a meat business in Bisbee, then founded a meat packing business in Phoenix which made him wealthy. His wife Della subsequently married William Stuart, publisher of the Prescott Courier. She bought Jerome radio station KCRJ from Charles R. Robinson.

Elijah H. Witherill: Referred to many times in early writings on Jerome as operator of Witherill station at base of Black Hills on the road to Jerome from Prescott.

Paul Smyley: Operated Annex Saloon in late nineties. He married Emma Rucker in 1898; she was captain of a Salvation army group, and refused Smyly's bid for her hand until he gave up the saloon business. He operated a bottling works in Jerome for years, and later cigar stores and pool halls in Jerome and Clarkdale.

Thomas B. Jones: Came to Jerome in 1905, worked in New York Store until with C. V. Brockway he founded the Brockway-Jones dry goods and furnishings store in 1910. He was active in civic affairs, a strong church member and a campaigner for prohibition for Jerome. He married Elizabeth Herdman, daughter of a pioneer United Verde employee. When Clarkdale was founded he opened a business in that town.

Charles T. Jolley: Started his Jerome career as clerk at the Montana Hotel in 1905. Later he took over the real estate and insurance business of Charles Lynch. Married Katherine Dicus in 1905. In 1914 sold his Jerome business to Norman F. Wykoff, and joined Thomas B. Jones as partner in Jones-Jolly Company at Clarkdale.

S. S. Ballard: Prominent as a jeweler in Jerome in first and second decades.

Charles R. Ewing: Was employed in the United Verde mine in 1905. In 1907 with Charles E. "Boney" Hughes, he established the transfer and livery business of Ewing & Hughes, known as the Jerome Transfer Company. In 1905 he married Miss Helen Boone of St. Louis. A son Charles (Carlos) studied law and became county attorney of Yavapai County. Charles E. Ewing died in 1934 at age 72.

Charles E. Hughes: Born in Ohio, "Boney" Hughes first reached Jerome in 1893 at age 17. He worked intermittently for the United Verde until he joined Charles R. Ewing in the transfer and livery business. This firm remained in business until gasoline power replaced horses and mules. Hughes then entered the insurance business. The name "Boney" was an abbreviation of "Boneytail," a name given by fishing pals. A fish called boneytail abounded in the Verde River. Colorful of language, Boney loved practical jokes and frequently indulged in them. He was married to Bertha Rucker Jacques in 1916. He died in Jerome in 1957. His widow is still numbered among Jerome's best known pioneers.

Joseph and Jacob Mingus: These brothers settled in the Black Hills area around 1880, and took up land at the western base of Mingus Mountain later acquired by Elijah Witherill. When mining and smelting activities started at Jerome they set up a sawmill on the mountain which came to bear their name.

George E. McMillan: Born in Illinois in 1879, he came to Arizona in 1900. He worked as an engineer on the narrow gauge line from Jerome Junction to Jerome until 1912, then transferred to the V. T. & S. railroad at Clarkdale. He drove the first of the big Mallets into Jerome in 1920. In 1921 he joined W. P. Scott in the undertaking and household furnishing business, and he was still in that business when he died in 1961, at age 81.

Thomas Jacobs: A native of Kentucky, he was a member of the well known operating crew of the United Verde and Pacific Railroad, serving as a conductor. When the narrow gauge line was abandoned he became a conductor on the Santa Fe branch line from Drake to Clarkdale. He worked at the United Verde mine during the depression. He died in 1944 at age 77.

George Haskins: He was born in Illinois, and took employment as an engineer on the United Verde & Pacific road in 1902. In 1914 he was transferred to the Verde Tunnel & Smelter road and drove the broad gauge locomotives until his retirement in 1938. He died in 1952 at age 81.

Alvin L. Reese: Chemist, merchant, banker, Al Reese was widely known in Jerome and the Verde Valley. About 1900 he entered the employ of the United Verde, and while Senator Clark's Iron King mine and smelter operated he was chemist at the plant at Macdonald, south of Jerome. For many years he was chief chemist for the United Verde at Clarkdale. Upon retirement he moved with his family to California.

W. P. Scott: Best known as Jerome's undertaker, he came to Jerome in its early days. He established a household furnishings business also, and with George E. McMillan as partner operated the firm until his death.

Val Harris: Operator of the Jerome Mercantile Company, he was prominent in Jerome business circles prior to the depression. At a time when the Jerome volunteer fire department needed reorganization, he was made chief and helped to build it into a highly efficient fire fighting unit. He retired to California.

The Rucker family: Conrad Rucker came to Jerome in 1897, followed by his family of ten. He was Jerome's superintendent of streets after the town's incorporation, and his son Ed was town clerk. Bertha Rucker Hughes is the only surviving member of the family.

Men involved in Jerome's town government stand in front of the temporary post office building on April 2, 1900. (Standing, left to right) E. P. Couger, W. D. McKinnon, Dr. Myron Carrier, Alex Lyons, William Howard, Parkinson, Charles E. Hughes, Billy Munds. (Sitting, left to right) Phil Boyd, T. N. Brown.

APPENDIX B.

Professional Men

In this section will be found the names of most of Jerome's early day physicians, dentists, and lawyers.

THE DOCTORS

The old time residents of Jerome had a special niche in their memories for their doctors, and the mining companies treated them well and provided them up-to-date facilities. During its life the United Verde had four hospitals, each larger and better equipped than its predecessor.

Dr. Myron A. Carrier

This well-known pioneer was the first to actively practice medicine in Jerome, arriving in 1881 even before the camp had a name. He had served in the Civil War and spent time in Libby prison. Lacking funds for the medical training to which he aspired, he traveled by wagon train to Utah, successfully engaged in trapping, and returned to the East with the means to study for a medical degree. After practicing for a time in Michigan he came to Jerome, where he made himself a part of the community by marrying Meloma Munds, daughter of William Munds. The couple had three daughters; one married Dr. Lee A. Hawkins, Jerome dentist; another became Mrs. William Loy of Oak Creek; the third, Mrs. Iva Carrier Shaw of California has furnished the Jerome Historical Society and this writer with valuable material concerning Jerome's early days.

Dr. Carrier spent his last years in Camp Verde, having to leave the high altitude of Jerome because of a heart condition. He died in 1907.

Dr. Charles Winter Woods

One of Jerome's most colorful characters, Dr. Woods lived and practiced in Jerome for a longer period than any of its other doctors. He resided there continuously from 1894 to his death in 1937 at age 83.

Jerome's first hospital (top left), built in 1894 and destroyed in the 1898 fire, is the three-story building behind Con O'Keefe's store. Building with arches in center of photograph (top right) is Jerome's second hospital, built in 1889, later renovated into the Hampton House, a hotel for miners. The third United Verde Hospital (lower left), built in 1917 and converted to the United Verde Clubhouse in 1927. The fourth United Verde Hospital (bottom right), built in 1927.

He was born in Tennessee, but he spent his youth in New Orleans, where he became a driver for and an aid to a doctor. He showed such adaptability that his employer encouraged him to take medical training. He did take a short course in medicine and surgery in a New York eclectic college.

Woods was an Octoroon, and he felt he would find better acceptance away from the south. He came to Arizona. He had not yet become located when in 1892 he found work as a laborer on a freight transfer gang at Jerome Junction. When a workman had a leg crushed in an accident, Woods took charge, amputated the leg, and did such a good job of it that H. J. Allen was impressed, brought the young man to Jerome and placed him in charge of the United Verde's new hospital. It was said that Allen had to use his considerable influence in Phoenix to persuade the territorial medical board to issue him a certificate to practice, but a few years later Woods was appointed to membership on the board. He remained the United Verde's chief surgeon until 1906. He then set up a private practice, which he pursued in a rather desultory way. He was married to Elvia Fazell, a San Francisco opera singer, musician and orchestra conductor of French training. She survived him.

Dr. L. P. Kaull

A graduate of the Kansas City Medical College, Dr. Kaull served as assistant to Dr. Woods and Dr. Murietta, whom he followed as chief surgeon at the United Verde Hospital. He resigned in the early twenties and moved to California.

He died in 1923 from the effects of a self-administered lethal drug.

Dr. Alfred J. Murietta

He received his medical training in California, and after a term of practice there came to Jerome as a replacement for Dr. Woods as chief surgeon for the United Verde Hospital. He held this position successfully for ten years, when he resigned to take up work as a specialist in his native state.

While in Jerome he purchased and operated the Red Cross drug store. He admitted to a probable common ancestry with the famed outlaw, Joaquin Murietta.

Dr. Arthur A. Carlson

Dr. Carlson was a graduate of the University of California Medical School in 1910. He was physician for work crews of the Santa Fe railroad when it completed laying rail into Clarkdale in 1912. He then joined the medical staff of the United Verde Copper Company under Dr. Kaull. When Kaull left, Carlson replaced him as chief surgeon, a post he held until 1945, when he resigned to become chief surgeon-administrator of the Marcus J. Lawrence Memorial Hospital at Cottonwood. He resigned in 1951 to enter private practice in Phoenix.

Dr. Carlson was active in Jerome civic affairs. He served on the city council for three terms, one as mayor. He was the inspiration for the organization of the Verde Valley Welfare Association during the depression, the target being the underprivileged young. His medical and surgical skills were administered without charge. He died in Phoenix in 1962.

Dr. James R. Moore

One of the best known of the Jerome physicians, Dr. Moore received his training at the Western Reserve Medical School at Cleveland and the University of Southern California Medical School at Los Angeles. In 1916 he was employed by the medical department of the Cananea Consolidated Copper Company at Sonora, Mexico, and in World War I he was a captain in the U. S. Army medical corps in France.

After the war he served as physician for the United Verde Extension Mining Company, then for the United Verde. He served at an American Mission Hospital in Egypt and at Muskingum College in Ohio, then returned to Jerome and the United Verde. Subsequently he was appointed superintendent of the Arizona State Hospital, then served as medical director for the Arizona State Industrial Commission and also of the Blue Cross and Blue Shield.

Dr. Louis E. Walsh

The older of two brothers who practiced in Jerome, Dr. Louis Walsh was born in 1882 in Ontario, Canada. His parents were United States citizens. He received his elementary and high school education in Michigan, and when he decided to become a doctor he chose the University of Michigan Medical College in which to train. He received his degree in 1916, and shortly thereafter accepted a post on the medical staff of the United Verde hospital in Jerome.

Dr. Louis liked Jerome and its inhabitants. One of them he liked so well he married her—Marie Sullivan, daughter of hotel man John Sullivan, the year after his arrival. The couple had three children. Richard, Patricia, and Louis, and also raised John Sullivan's daughter Mary after the death of her mother.

Dr. Walsh made the Verde Valley his permanent home, and remained with the copper company's medical department at Jerome and Clarkdale until his early death in 1934.

Dr. James Malcolm Walsh

He was born in Canada in Prescott, Ontario, as was his brother Louis; his parents were Richard and Harriet Walsh, United States citizens. The year of his birth was 1886. After grade and high school in Michigan and college in Ontario, he attended the University of Michigan Medical College, from which he graduated in 1908. He came to Jerome to enter the service of the United Verde hospital in 1918.

Dr. Malcolm, as he was known, served a term as president of the Yavapai County Medical Society, and was active in the Arizona Medical Association. In 1958 he received a plaque from the association honoring his fifty years service. He married Helen Marie Reese, daughter of a Jerome pioneer. A son, John Donald, is a resident of Jerome, a past president of the Jerome Historical Society, and is active in civic affairs.

Dr. James Malcolm Walsh died in 1967.

Dr. Robert K. Hilton

A graduate of the University of Chicago's Rush Medical College, Dr. Hilton came to the Verde Valley in 1929 as a physician for the United Verde Extension, and later became attached to the United Verde medical staff. Now practicing in Litchfield Park, Arizona, he is a widely known and respected member of the medical profession.

During the life of the Jerome mines many other doctors served the people of Jerome. We give the names of well-known men of medicine and surgery who practiced in Jerome during the first four decades of the century:

THEY CAME TO JEROME

Doctors E. T. Cody, J. F. Coleman, J. A. Griffen, M. S. Gaede, F. J. Hart, C. C. Hedberg, E. B. Jolley, J. Ketcherside, H. W. Levengood, J. K. McDonnell, F. C. Norman, F. L. Powers, A. J. Rosenberry, Riley Shrum, R. T. Thigpen, J. W. Witten; and several others whose initials are not at hand—Doctors Beardslee, Clark, Livingston, Lowry, Murphy and Phillips.

THE DENTISTS

Dr. Lee A. Hawkins

In asking old timers about the most interesting characters of early Jerome, all placed Dr. Hawkins at or near the head of the list. Of a pioneer family and a real pioneer in his own right, largely self-trained, he was a colorful individual and widely known.

He was born in Missouri in 1867, and traveling behind an ox team came with his parents to the Verde Valley when still a small boy. The family settled at Peck's Lake in the early seventies. M. A. Ruffner also lived at the lake, and often when he rode up the trail to work his claims, Lee would ride behind him and spend the day among the pines.

He was hardly of age when he settled in Jerome and opened a dental office. People liked to twit him about his scant schooling in dentistry; a common story was that his first patients were horses. Later he took training at a dental school.

Lee Hawkins developed into a pretty good dentist, but he liked to experiment. After killing the nerve in an aching tooth he would fill the cavity by driving in a cactus thorn. In large cavities he would put in a filling of asphalt. He invented a machine to cast inlays, and equipped a little machine shop next to his office in which to build it. For some reason it didn't work.

With Walter Miller he bought the first motor car to appear in Jerome. He was a popular member of a number of organizations.

He married a daughter of Dr. Myron A. Carrier, Jerome's first doctor. He had a son who was accidentally killed in Hawaii.

He lived out his life in Jerome. He died in 1932 at age 65, and was buried with his folks in the Cottonwood cemetery.

Many other dentists came and went in Jerome. Among them were Doctors A. N. Cooper, F. J. Harvey, W. P. Gibbes, James Dickson,

M. O. Dumas, James Snipes, and two sons of pioneers, George H. McMillan and Joseph T. Pecharich. Though Jerome long since has become a barren field for professional men, Dr. Joe Pecharich remained in the Verde valley. With his brother Dr. Ray he built a dental clinic in Cottonwood, which remains a busy place.

ATTORNEYS AT LAW

John W. Ross

Born in Arkansas in 1866, he opened an office in Prescott in 1892, and established residence in Jerome in 1897. He remained there only a few years.

Heyward M. Gibbes

This lawyer came to Jerome in the late nineties from Virginia. His wife was of the Langhorne family and a cousin of Lady Astor.

Gibbes became Jerome's first city attorney in 1898. He held the office until 1906, when the council abolished it, then reestablished it and appointed another lawyer. In 1908, with several other lawyers practicing in Jerome, Gibbes felt the field was overcrowded and with his family returned east. The field was overcrowded there too, and in 1910 he returned to Jerome. In 1912 he was made city attorney and was reappointed in 1914 and 1916.

Carl M. Heim

Heim commenced the practice of law in Jerome in 1908, and sought a niche as the friend of the working man. He became associated with Roy W. Moon in the real estate and insurance business. As related elsewhere in this book he was shot in the head at the time of Guy Bailey's murder and lost an eye.

Charles H. Rutherford

This attorney came to Jerome in 1908 and through his activities soon became well known. He was elected to the state senate, and traveled to boost the sale of liberty bonds during World War I, making appearances as "Senator Rutherford of Arizona."

He served as city attorney in 1908, 1910, 1922 and 1924. He left Jerome in 1924 and established a practice in Phoenix.

THEY CAME TO JEROME

Norman F. Wykoff

He came to Jerome early in the first decade, worked for the United Verde, and among other activities engaged in the real estate business, for a time in association with S. F. Denison. After studying law and practicing for awhile in Jerome he moved to Prescott, then to Glendale, which city he served for a period as city attorney.

John L. Sullivan

Son of John M. Sullivan, pioneer hotel man, he opened a law office in Jerome in 1917. With a bent for politics, he successfully sought the office of county attorney in 1920, and in 1924 won the office of the state's attorney general. After he left that office he continued the practice of law in Phoenix.

Perry M. Ling

A son of Reese M. Ling, a prominent attorney who had served Jerome in its fight to retain its status as an incorporated town, he chose Jerome in which to set up a practice. He became city attorney in 1924, a post which he held for several terms. He subsequently established a practice in Phoenix.

Other Attorneys

Among others who practiced in Jerome in its earlier years were T. R. Collins, Parkinson & Von Schriltz, Roger O'Malley, Norton & Carlisle, and Lewis A. Bunte.

* * *

APPENDIX C.

Some Who Opened the Golden Door

Though we cannot give them all, we give here the names of some of the immigrants, who having entered a new land through the golden door, succeeded in becoming well known in Jerome. In many cases their children entered business, the arts and the professions throughout the Southwest and spread the family names.

The Slavs: Blazina, Dragich, Delovich, Cvijanovich, Katich, Knezovich, Kauzlarich, Kovacovich, Krmpotich, Krznarich, Livkovich, Minerich, Muretic, Pecharich, Radakovich, Radick, Starkovich, Svob.

A number of the men in the above and following groups were supervisory officials at the United Verde and other mining plants.

The Italians: Bechetti, Beneitone, Bertino, Bonadillo, Bratazani, De-Felippi, DeZolt, Issoglio, Mariani, Mongini, Peila, Pozzobon, Selna, Tavasci, Tamietti, Veretto.

The Irish: Bradley, Connolly, Harrington, Haskins, O'Keefe, Ryan, Shea, Sullivan.

The Mexicans: Tisnado, Rivera, Miramon, Santillan, Guitierrez, Pecina, Mendez, Paz, Cota, Pena, Quijada, Rodriguez, Ochoa, Dominguez, Sanora, Villa.

Others: Names of many others who attained a degree of prominence in Jerome will be found in preceding sections of this book.

Of the few French speaking immigrants, well-known were the names of Bots, Rampont, Marembert and Naussin. Of the Germans there were Rothermel, Thorbeck, Vogel, Fischer, Schott and Wiegand.

There were Chinese in Jerome from the earliest days, whose presence disturbed the citizens from time to time. None of them labored; all engaged in private enterprise, almost entirely restaurant and laundry operation. An exception was Charley Hong, who not only operated restaurants but owned a ranch in the valley. He was a member of a Protestant church and took part to some extent in public affairs.

Opium dens in Jerome were frequently raided by the law, but they persisted.

169

Aerial view of Jerome, circa 1930 (Jerome Historical Society)

There were never more than two or three Japanese in Jerome. When a Flagstaff businessman tried to settle a colony of Japanese on a ranch on the Verde River after the First World War, the three valley American Legion posts led a movement in opposition, and made so much noise the project was abandoned.

In addition to the immigrants, in the early days a small colony of Apache Indians built their wickiups on the outskirts of Jerome. A few of the men worked as laborers; some of the women performed domestic chores. Long remembered was Apache Susie; she did laundry, her man delivered and collected the money. Once when he spent all he collected Susie skewered him with a butcher knife. Maggie Hayes was another Indian woman who worked in Jerome in the early days and lived out her life in the valley; she was well educated, and reminiscences of her life on and off the reservation were published.

Three Apache scouts of more than local fame frequented Jerome: Major Smyly and John Ketcham, who participated in the capture of Geronimo, and Jim Ketchum, who served under General Crook as a special Indian policeman. These men all proudly wore their decorations, and each lived to an advanced age.

Yee Hang Song, Chinese proprietor of the English Kitchen, standing in the doorway of his restaurant during the bleak years of the 1960's. (Jerome Historical Society, Cannel Col.)

171

APPENDIX D.

Businesses and Services, Saloons and Mines

In this section are listed the names of those individuals, firms and corporations who were progressive enough to advertise or prominent enough to find frequent mention in Jerome's newspapers from 1895 to 1935. There were others some of whom have been mentioned in earlier chapter of this book. The memories of others still have vanished with the mountain winds.

Names in parentheses indicate operators subsequent to the original owners.

Allison's Candy Factory; Mrs. A. Ananients, dressmaking; All Nations Meat Market; Arizona Market, Roy Dunn; A. N. Aveldson, photographer.

S. S. Ballard, jeweler; The Bank of Arizona; the Bank of Jerome; Bartlett Hotel, E. C. Bartlett; The Beauty Parlor; Beck Drug Company; Bell Restaurant, Lena; Black Canyon Stage Line; Black House—25¢ a night, C. Rucker; Bon Ton Chop House, Jap Charley; Boston Store, L. Farrage; Boyd Hotel, Kitty and Harry Crain; M. J. Brennan, photographer; Brisley & Tarr, drugs, Harry Brisley and Elwin F. Tarr; Brockway-Jones Company, dry goods and clothing, C. V. Brockway and Thomas B. Jones; J. M. Brown, barber; Lewis A. Bunte, attorney; John Burke, real estate.

California Restaurant, Jack Sims; E. W. Carroll, broker; Central Pharmacy; Champion Shoe Shop; City Transfer Company, John Goodwin and William Holliday; Clarkdale Dairy; J. H. Clinkscales, business block; Coliseum Theater, William Haskins, Phil Pecharich; Connor the Tailor; Connor Cafe; Connor Hotel, Dave Connor; George H. Cook, jeweler; Copper City Plumbing, Matt Shea.

Roy Dale's Electric Shop; Dashaway Livery Stable, Scott, Moore and Nevins; Davenport Cafe; Denison & Wykoff, insurance; Dicus Blacksmith Shop, H. E. Dicus; Dicus Garage, H. E. Dicus; M. F. Dicus, plumber and tinner; Dunn and Lipsey, men's clothing.

Electric Theater, R. A. Smith (Clark); Elite Restaurant, Charley

Sam and Dees Lui; English Kitchen, Charley Hong (and many successors); Carl A. Enderle, plumbing; Arthur Estey, plumbing; Exchange Restaurant, Charley Hong.

Fain Brothers, meats; Ruth Fallon, dressmaking; Fashion Shoppe, flowers; Louis Ferber, real estate, investments; Fischer's Confectionery, Gottlieb Fischer; Fountain Pool Hall, Mike Dragich; Thomas Fowler, vegetables and fruits; F. L. France, real estate.

Henry Galbraith, contractor; Goldberg Brothers, men's furnishings; Golden Rule Store, Peter Gordon, dry goods and furnishings; H. J. Gottlieb, photo gallery; Grand Central Hotel, Mrs. Marian Keith, (Mrs. H. N. Crain), (Frank DeZolt); Grand Central Restaurant, Walter Fallis; Grand View Barber Shop, Wm. Parker & Co.; Grand View Hotel, J. E. Meguire.

Haff & Colwell, mining engineers; J. C. Halstead Lumber Company; Hamilton Grocery; Haskell & Kirwagen, ranch and orchards; Jim Haskins, super-service station; L. E. Hesla, jeweler; Hi-Grade Studio, A. S. Houghton, photographer; The Home Company, Charles E. Hughes, real estate and insurance; Home Restaurant, Mrs. Kenny; Charles Hong, restaurant; Hong & Gillette, dairy; Hooker Transfer Lines, Charles Hooker; Hooker & Page, livery; The Hub, Curt Sterrman, men's clothing; Hull & Company, general merchandise, lumber; Hustler Cafe, Jack Sims.

Independent Barber Shop, J. H. Cleary; Independent Meat Company; H. Ingraham, violin teacher; Issoglio & Moore, Louis Issoglio and R. E. Moore, cigar store and pool; Ivester Electric Company.

Jerome Baking Company, Thorbeck; Jerome Battery & Electric Company; Jerome Cigar Store, F. L. France; Jerome Cash & Carry; Jerome Chamber of Mines; Jerome Chop House, Ti Sing; Jerome Coca Cola Bottling Works; Jerome Dairy, J. F. Dwyer, (Fred Mickle); Jerome Drug Company, Dr. A. J. Murrieta, H. T. Jackson, manager, (Roddan & Gassaway); Jerome Hotel, Rothermel & Parker; Jerome Garage & Machine Shop, H. E. Dicus and John E. Wagner; Jerome Garage, Nash cars; Jerome Jewelry & Music Store; Jerome Livery & Express, T. M. Cavenaugh; Jerome Lumber Company, J. F. Mullin, W. F. Montgomery, L. W. Pugh, A. D. Hayes; Jerome Lumber Yard, T. H. Brown; Jerome Meat Company, Ed E. Tovrea (Tovrea & Clay) (P. T. Hurley) (W. H. Cox); Jerome Mercantile Company, dry goods, clothing, Val Harris; Jerome Plumbing & Sheet Metal Company, I.

H. Nihell; Jerome Pool Hall; Jerome Produce Company; Jerome Realty & Insurance Company; R. Moore and Carl M. Heim; Jerome Sanitary Laundry; Jerome Tailoring Company; Jerome Transfer Company, hauling, bus service, livery, Ewing & Hughes; J. & S. Barber Shop; Jim the Cobbler; Allen Johnson, blacksmith; Johnson & Dodsworth, masonry contractors; Charles T. Jolly, real estate and insurance; Jones Auditing Company, E. H. and Charles F. Jones; Frank E. Jordan, painter and paper hanger.

Antone Kauzlerich, groceries and meats; KCRJ Radio Station, Charles R. Robinson; Mrs. Keeler, dressmaker; Kentucky Bowling Alley, Fred Whitaker; Kovacovich Mercantile Company, Emil Kovacovich, general merchandise; John E. Kunst, architect and engineer.

Landon & Berman, hardware and furnishings; Leland Hotel, Mrs. Charles Sutter; R. Allyn Lewis, stocks and bonds; Liberty Theater, Phil Pecharich; Mike Loftus, barber; Lyons & Knoblock, groceries; A. H. Lyons, general merchandise; Charles T. Lynch, real estate and insurance; Lyric Theater, Johnson Brothers.

Marques & Beltran, cigars, pool, barber shop; Mendez Transfer Company, firewood; Doane and Horace Merrill, general merchandise; Horace Merrill, real estate and insurance; Fred Mickle, dairy; Miner Barber Shop, J. L. Buck; Miners Furniture & Hardware, Thomas A. Miller; Miners Cafe; Miners Meat Market; Miners Grocery; Minerva Cafe; Mingus Amusement Company; Mitchell Drug Store; Modern Cafe, Johnson Brothers; Roy W. Moon, real estate and insurance; R. E. Moore Company, insurance; Myers Drug Store, Walter and Dana Myers.

Nevada Cafe, Carr & Engelech; Frank Nevin, undertaker; New Meat Market, Nic Radakovich, John M. Sullivan, Joe Pecharich; New State Garage, Matt Shea and Phil Pecharich (Fred Whitaker and Maurice Goodwin); New York Pool Hall; New York Restaurant; New York Store, dry goods, clothing: I. Laskin, (William Lubin), (Nathan Shutz).

O. K. Meat Market, G. W. Hart; O. K. Pool and Billiard Rooms; Con O'Keefe, clothing, furnishings, general merchandise; John Opman, real estate and insurance.

Palace Livery Stable; Paramount Beauty Parlor; Paz & Cota, groceries and general merchandise, pool hall; Pena's Place; J. C. Penney Company; Perry Photo Gallery, Oliver Hazard Perry; Pioneer Truck Company, Joseph Lieberman; The Popular Store; Porter's Grocery,

Robert K. Porter; Porter's Home Bakery; Post Office Cigar Store, Campbell & Myers, (R. A. Smith), (E. W. Carroll), (Fred Mickle), (Fred Boyd & Matt Mungovan), (Harry Mitchell); Post Office Pharmacy, Bernard MacDonald; Pruitt & Deane, plumbing; James Prosser, contractor.

The Racket Store; Radley Transfer Company, J. W. Radley & Sons; Tony Ranwick, tailor; Red Cross Drug Store, E. F. Tarr; Reese & Amster, garage and machine shop, Harry Amster and Kent Reese; Will Reese Apartments; Reliable Jewelry Store, Ernest Emanuel; Ritz Barber Shop; Ritz Theater; W. E. Rhodes, private dining room; Charles E. Robinson, jeweler; Mrs. J. K. Ruff, ladies wear.

St. Elmo Restaurant, Jap Charley; St. Elmo Tonsorial Parlor, Charles Matthewson; Saratoga Restaurant, Mrs. Carr; Sanitary Laundry, William Conklin; Charles Sauer, contractor; W. P. Scott, undertaker, home furnishings; Scott & Ballard, brokers, J. C. Scott and S. S. Ballard; Scott & McMillan, undertakers, home furnishings; Scott & Nevin, undertakers; Scott & Williams, undertakers, home furnishings; Selna's Grocery, Virgil Selna; Selna & Kovacovich, groceries, Virgil Selna and Emil Kovacovich; Senate Restaurant, Hon Lee; Service Drug Company; Charley Shaw Restaurant; D. J. Shea Company, general merchandise, Dan, Matt, Tim and Dennis Shea, M. J. Bradley and John P. Connolly; Matt Shea, cigars and tobaccos; Shea & Ryan, plumbing, Con Shea and Thomas Ryan; Harry M. Simington, mineral surveyor (U.S. Deputy); Paul Smyly Bottling Works; Paul Smyly, cigars, tobacco, soft drinks, news; Star Restaurant, Dae Buck Hong; Starr Jewelry; R. S. Sturmer, grocer, baker, hardware; Sunset Dairy.

A. P. Thompson, mining geologist; Thorbeck's Bakery, Joseph and August Thorbeck; Tipton Motor Company, A. R. Tipton; The Toggery, Harry Krotinger.

Union Meat Market; L. L. Upson, tinsmith and plumber.

R. Vannie & Company, sea foods; Verde District Dairy, Joe Bratizani & Company; Verde Drug Store; Verde Motor Company; Verde Valley Stage Company; Vienna Cafe, Mrs. Frisch.

Wah Kee Chop House; A. E. Weidman Company, brokers; Charles D. Willard, dairy; F. Woods, plumbing; N. F. Wykoff, real estate and insurance; Norman F. Wykoff, attorney at law.

Yavapai Drug Store; Yavapai Electric Works; Ye Olde Candy

Shoppe, Hoyt & Young; Young-Hansohn Company, variety store, H. V. Young and A. C. Hansohn.

Zaragosa Theater, Santiago Tisnado.

*　　*　　*

When the bonanza discovery of the United Verde Extension Mining Company occurred midway of the second decade, it triggered a boom the like of which had not been seen before in northern Arizona. All lands not previously located in the Verde Mining area, over the mountain and clean down to the Verde River, were filed on as mining claims. Dozens of "mining" companies were formed, a goodly number legitimate but many for wildcatting purposes. Below is a list of the majority of Verde district mining companies, as mentioned in local journals through the years, though there were others which shunned publicity locally and peddled their gilded certificates in other parts of the country. In these days such promotions would not be allowed, but the wildcatters had a free hand then and made the most of it.

Arkansas & Arizona.

Black Hills Copper.

Calumet & Jerome; Clark Jerome; Cleopatra Copper; Cobrita Verde; Consolidated King & Columbia; Copper Chief; Copper Chief Extension.

Dundee Arizona.

Eureka Gold & Copper.

Gadsden Copper; Grand Island; Green Monster; Great Verde Extension.

Haynes Copper; Hull Copper.

Illinois & Jerome; Iron King.

Jerome Copper Mining; Jerome Daisy; Jerome Metals; Jerome Del Monte; Jerome North Star; Jerome Pacific; Jerome Portland; Jerome St. Louis; Jerome Superior; Jerome Verde; Jerome Verde Contact; Jerome Victor; Jerome Victor Extension; Jerome Yaeger.

Lone Pine Verde; Louisiana-Arizona.

Mescal Mining; Michigan Verde; Mingus Mountain Copper; Monster Chief.

Pittsburgh Jerome.

Shea Copper; Squaw Peak Mining; Sunrise Group.

Three Medals; Two Republics.

United Jerome; United Verde; United Verde Consolidated; United Verde Extension; United Verde Junior.

Venture Hill; Verde Apex; Verde Central; Verde Central Extension; Verde Chief; Verde Chief Extension; Verde Combination; Verde Copper; Verde Copper Development; Verde Grande; Verde Hercules; Verde King; Verde Monster; Verde Queen; Verde Squaw; Verde Syndicate; Verde Victor; Verde Victor Extension; Verde Mining & Milling.

Washburn Group.

Yaeger Copper.

The people of Jerome had more than thirty years in which to openly slake their thirsts for alcoholic beverages before the state prohibition law went into effect in 1915. The saloons listed below were those which, during that period, sought or were given publicity in the newspapers.

Annex Saloon, Charles R. Fiske.

Billy's Place, William Haskins, (Bracken & McMahon); Balkan Saloon, Nick Radakovich, (Tamietti & Bertini).

Connor Hotel Bar, Dave Connor; Club Saloon, M. P. Tighe, (Frank Rainey).

Elite Saloon, J. E. Lanham; Exchange Saloon, Dave Connor.

The Fashion, Hoover & Cordiner. (John Keller & Company), (Alex Cordiner).

Fountain Saloon, Louis Issoglio.

Junction Saloon, Alex Duff.

Kentucky Liquor House, J. Weinberger, (Fischer & Altman).

La Embarcacion Saloon, Bernardo Quijada.

Manhattan Saloon, Fred Ullman, (Matt Shea); Miners Exchange, Pete McIntyre; Miners Union Saloon; Montana Saloon, Sullivan & Harrington.

Otto's Place, Otto Vogel.

Paris Saloon, Frank DeZolt.

Reception Saloon, Tom Dolovich.

The St. Elmo, McFarland & Hooker, (Charles Hooker), (Gibson & Johnson); Senate Saloon, William T. Neff; Shea's Place, Dan J.

Shea; Star Saloon, Sparkes & Conway; Stone Saloon, Dave Connor; Sullivan Hotel Bar, John M. Sullivan.

J. P. Taggart Liquor Store; Turf Saloon, Joe Pecharich and Nic Radakovich.

Ward & Cole Saloon; Wigwam Saloon, Theo Marambert; Working-man's Saloon, John J. Becker.

Old timers declare that Jerome had its own "Bucket of Blood" saloon, but no published reference has been found regarding a saloon of that name.

PHOTOGRAPH BY STALEY

Jerome, circa 1927, at its peak population of nearly 15,000.
(Jerome Historical Society, Franquero Col.)

APPENDIX E.

Jerome's Public Servants

Early attempts to incorporate Jerome as a municipality failed because of the opposition of George W. Hull, the largest individual property owner in the camp, and his supporters. But after the big fire of 1898 the clamor for fire laws, an adequate water supply, and more fire fighting equipment, became demanding.

Though Hull had sold many of the lots on which business houses and residences had been built, the deeds he gave covered only surface rights to a depth of twenty-five feet, all mineral rights being retained. Therefore, Hull was able to claim that a petition for incorporation without his signature could not represent a majority of the real estate which had been proposed for inclusion within the town boundaries.

During that period Hull was spending considerable time in the East, beginning the promotion of his United Verde Extension Gold, Silver & Copper Mining Company and attempting to obtain a divorce from his wife, a resident of Rhode Island. On such a trip in 1898 a petition contaning signatures of a majority of the individuals owning ground in the town's center was presented to the county board of supervisors, requesting incorporation. The board issued a certificate of incorporation and appointed councilmen and other officers to serve until the first town election.

Incensed at this coup, upon his return Hull entered suit in the Yavapai County superior court to have the order for incorporation invalidated. Though he carried the contest to the territorial supreme court, the action of the supervisors was upheld.

The following freeholders became the first councilmen of the new Town of Jerome; William Munds, mayor, and Michael J. Bradley, Arthur Cordiner, Doane Merrill, and R. S. Sturmer. Appointments: R. E. McDowell, clerk; Frank Ferguson, marshal; Thomas Miller, deputy marshal; F. H. Perkins, building inspector; J. C. Duff, street commissioner, and Dr. M. A. Carrier, health officer.

In 1899 the town held its first election, at which all councilmen and appointees were returned to office. Subsequent elections were held in even numbered years, beginning in 1900.

The town's first election ordinance provided that not only the councilmen but most of the other offices were elective. This practice was maintained until after statehood, when all offices except the council members were by statute made appointive, with tenure subject to the will of the council.

The council early established a rule, maintained to this day, that the candidate for councilmen who received the most votes was to be named the mayor.

At the 1900 election the following candidates were chosen; E. A. Tovrea, mayor; M. R. Beagley; M. J. Bradley, Charles Hooker and Rudolph Rothermel, councilmen; S. L. Heslet, Clerk; James F. Roberts, marshal, and Fred Hawkins, deputy marshal; and Dr. Charles W. Woods, health officer.

The 1902 election brought out an opposition ticket; the labor party ran candidates against the "establishment," called the citizens' party. Elected were Walter C. Miller; mayor; Dave Connor, S. E. Garrett, William Parks and Rudolph Rothermel, the only candidate of the labor party to make the grade. Other officers were S. L. Heslet, clerk, James F. Roberts, marshal, Fred Hawkins, deputy marshal, Conrad Rucker, Street superintendent, H. M. Gibbes, attorney, and Dr. J. Coleman, health officer.

The 1904 election was held with no opposition to the citizens' party, with the following results: George W. Hull, mayor, and Fred Ullman, M. J. Bradley, Rudolph Rothermel and M. J. Foley, councilmen. R. A. Smith was named clerk, James F. Roberts, marshal, Fred Hawkins, deputy marshal, H. M. Gibbes, attorney, Dr. J. Coleman, health officer, and Charles Rucker, superintendent of streets. Roberts resigned as marshal in 1904 and Fred Hawkins was appointed to replace him. R. D. Durain was his night deputy.

In the 1906 campaign a new party, the Progressive, appeared to oppose the Citizens', but they were defeated by a two to one margin. Elected: George W. Hull, mayor, with Horace F. Merrill, Harry E. Dicus, Charles Sutter and William Holliday for councilmen. Other officers: Fred Gorham, clerk, Fred Hawkins, marshal, Dr. J. W. Coleman, health officer, and J. C. Duff, street commissioner.

There was some opposition to Gibbes, and the council abolished the office of "city" attorney, then later re-established it and appointed Charles H. Rutherford, a newcomer who had made a favorable impression in Jerome.

Elected in 1908: George W. Hull, mayor; councilmen, Charles Sutter, Charles Hooker, Dave Connor and W. B. Cox. Other officers: Charles E. Hughes, clerk, Fred Hawkins, marshal, Charles King, deputy marshal, Charles H. Rutherford, attorney, Dr. A. J. Murietta, health officer, and W. S. Adams, city magistrate.

1910: David Connor, mayor; councilmen, Paul Smyly, S. S. Ballard, C. T. Jolly and John Lyons. Subsequently Lyons was disqualified, not being a freeholder, and Dave Connor resigned. Appointed to fill these vacancies were R. A. Williams and W. H. Cox. Other officers were R. C. Lane, clerk, Fred Hawkins, marshal, Charles King, deputy marshal, Charles H. Rutherford, attorney, and Dr. A. J. Murietta, health officer.

1912: R. C. Lane, mayor, with councilmen Joe Larson, R. A. Williams, Arthur C. Cordiner and John M. Goodwin. Other officers: John J. Harringson, clerk; Fred Hawkins, marshal; John Hudgens, deputy marshal; H. M. Gibbes, attorney, and S. F. Denison, magistrate. Early in 1912 R. C. Lane resigned from the council, having moved to Clarkdale to become manager of the United Verde's subsidiary companies headquartered at the valley town. The council appointed Dave Hopkins to fill the vacancy, and Goodwin was chosen mayor.

1914: Councilmen elected, John M. Goodwin, mayor, J. W. Radley, Joe Larson, Dave Hopkins and A. C. Cordiner. Other officers: Fred Whitaker, Clerk; Fred Hawkins, marshal; John Hudgens and H. W. Wilson, deputy marshals; H. M. Gibbes, attorney; Dr. A. J. Murietta, health officer; S. F. Denison, magistrate, and J. W. Hubbard, street supervisor.

1916: Councilmen elected, J. J. Cain, mayor, Nathan Shutz, H. E. Dicus, J. W. Radley, and W. P. Scott. Other officers: Fred Whitaker, clerk; Fred Hawkins, marshal; Hank Clift and B. G. Shepard, deputy marshals; H. M. Gibbes, attorney; Dr. A. J. Murietta, health officer, and Jake Weber, street supervisor. Deputy marshals Clift and Shepard were fired in August, 1916, and Monta Broaded and Charles Saunders appointed, together with John Lyons. Dr. Murietta resigned early in the year, and Dr. A. C. Carlson replaced him as health officer.

1918: Councilmen elected, James Presley, mayor, Dave Goodwin, A. D. Hayes, C. M. Thorpe, and Rudolph Rothermel. This Citizens' ticket was opposed by a full "People's" ticket, which got nowhere. Other officers: A. E. Weidman, clerk; Johns G. Crowley, marshal; W. S. Adams, police judge; Dr. A. C. Carlson, health officer; T. R. Macleod, engineer, and Charles Sauer, building inspector. Fred Hawkins did not serve again as an officer of the town of Jerome, but he was stationed in Jerome as a deputy by the county sheriff.

1920: From nine candidates for the office of councilman, the following were elected: Dr. A. C. Carlson, mayor; James F. Presley, R. E. Moore, Charles E. Hughes, and J. E. Wagner. Other officers: Ed Rucker, clerk; John G. Crowley, marshal (the council gave him the title of chief of police); D. L. Betts and W. S. Kirby, police officers, and Joe McCarthy, engineer. With the establishment of the office of chief of police, that officer was given authority to appoint his deputies, the council relinquishing that power.

1922: Councilmen elected without opposition; Robert K. Porter, mayor; J. E. Wagner, Charles E. Hughes, Dr. A. C. Carlson, and James F. Presley. Other officers; Ed Rucker, clerk, John G. Crowley, chief of police, Clyde B. Jones, police judge, James Hubbard, street superintendent, and Joseph McCarthy, city engineer.

1924: Councilmen elected without opposition; Milton Scott, mayor; Thomas A. Miller, James F. Presley, Robert K. Porter, and Frost L. Benham. Other officers, Robert E. Moore, clerk, John G. Crowley, chief of police, Charles E. Rutherford, attorney, and Dr. A. C. Carlson, health officer.

1926: Councilmen elected without opposition; John P. Connolly, mayor, Thomas A. Miller, Carl E. Mills, Milton W. Scott, and Frost L. Benham. Other officers: Robert E. Moore, clerk, John G. Crowley, chief of police, Perry M. Ling, attorney, Clyde B. Jones, police judge, Dr. C. C. Hedberg, health officer, and Charles Risinger, building inspector.

1928: Councilmen elected without opposition; Thomas A. Miller, mayor; Harry Mader, James Cheek, John P. Connolly, and Carl E. Mills. Other officers: Robert E. Moore, clerk, John G. Crowley, chief of police, and Perry M. Ling, attorney.

1930: Councilmen elected without opposition; Thomas A. Miller, mayor; Harry Mader, James Cheek, John F. Connolly, and Carl E. Mills. Other officers: Robert E. Moore, clerk, John G. Crowley, chief of police, and Perry M. Ling, attorney.

1932: Councilmen elected without opposition: Harry J. Mader, mayor; Ed Rucker, John F. Connolly, Thomas E. Miller, and Carl E. Mills. Other officers: Robert E. Moore, clerk, John G. Crowley, chief of police, and Perry M. Ling, attorney.

1934: This was the last election for councilman held in Jerome while the United Verde Copper Company remained under Clark ownership. In 1935 Phelps Dodge Corporation took control.

Councilmen elected without opposition: Thomas A. Miller, mayor; Harry J. Mader, Carl E. Mills, John P. Connolly, and Ed Rucker. John G. Crowley was reappointed chief of police, Perry M. Ling, city attorney, and Robert E. Moore remained the clerk.

First elected clerk in 1924, Moore was supported by the United Verde, and with this influence behind him he was then and for years to follow virtually the city manager of Jerome.

* * *

Jerome's postmasters: Following are the postmasters who have served Jerome up to the present time, with the years of their appointments and the names of the presidents who appointed them.

Frederick F. Thomas, 1883, Arthur; Frederick E. Murray, 1885, Cleveland; Doane Merrill, 1892, Harrison; Samuel F. Meguire, 1893, Harrison; Frank E. Jordan, 1897, Cleveland; Thomas E. Campbell, 1902, McKinley; Dan L. Robinson, 1908, T. Roosevelt; Frank E. Smith, 1909, Taft; W. S. Adams, 1913, Wilson; William E. Leonard, 1917, Wilson; Ross H. Cunningham, 1919, Wilson; Ethel Cunningham, 1936, F. Roosevelt; John E. Wagner, 1936, F. Roosevelt; Hazel D. Fredell, 1953, Eisenhower; Richard E. Lawrence, 1953, Eisenhower; Beverly J. Sullivan, 1964, Johnson.

Jerome's first justice of the peace was Major E. K. Otey, who held this county office until his death in 1908. L. B. St. James succeeded him, and officiated until 1907, when he resigned and left Jerome. W. S. Adams was appointed to fill his unexpired term, and was elected to the office in 1908. Other men to hold this office during the period covered by this book were M. Hawley, John J. Harrington, Frank Smith, and Clyde B. Jones.

The Jerome town council usually appointed the justice of the peace to act as city magistrate also.

INDEX

INDEX

INDEX

INDEX

189

INDEX

INDEX

INDEX

INDEX

INDEX

INDEX

INDEX

INDEX

INDEX

INDEX